THE CERTAINTY OF BEING LOVED

To

Anne-Marie Gustavson-Claverie
for her encouragement and support

and to

Sr Anne-Catherine Meyer OP
for her unstinting devotion
to the memory and message of Pierre Claverie OP

Martin McGee OSB

Foreword by Timothy Radcliffe OP

The Certainty of Being Loved

Pierre Claverie OP, 1938-1996

DOMINICAN PUBLICATIONS

First published (2021) by
Dominican Publications
42 Parnell Square
Dublin 1

ISBN 978-1-905604-44-9

British Library Cataloguing in Publications Data.
A catalogue record for this book is available
from the British Library.

Cover design by David Cooke

Printed in Ireland by
SPRINT-print, Dublin

Contents

Part 3 *Understanding Islam*

....

Acknowledgements

I WOULD like to thank all those who gave so generously of their time to help me write about Blessed Pierre Claverie OP. Anne-Marie Gustavson-Claverie, Pierre's sister, was unstinting in her support, making available photographs, hitherto unpublished letters from her brother and answering promptly all my questions. Sr Anne-Catherine Meyer OP was also incredibly generous with her time and encouragement. She readily made available photographs and the digitised version of Mgr Claverie's writings. Her devotion to keeping Pierre's memory alive knows no bounds.

Anne-Marie Claverie-Gustavson, Sr Anne-Catherine Meyer OP, Fr Jean-Jacques Pérennès OP, and Dom Luke Bell OSB all read carefully the first draft of my book, making many helpful corrections and suggestions. Mgr Henri Teissier, Mgr Claude Rault M. Afr., Fr Jean-Jacques Pérennès OP, Fr Thierry Becker and Anne-Marie Gustavson-Claverie all very kindly answered a questionnaire which I sent to them about Pierre. I am also grateful to Fr Timothy Radcliffe OP who wrote the foreword, and to Sr Mary Helen Jackson OC and Amilton Ary Fonseca Lopes who each forwarded an important article. Finally, my thanks go to Abbot Luke and my fellow monks at Worth Abbey for supporting my interest in the Algerian Church and its martyrs.

The many translations from French into English are my own.

....

Timeline

18 April 1936	Marriage of Étienne Claverie and Louise Maillard in the Church of St Vincent de Paul, Algiers
8 May 1938	Birth of Pierre Claverie
1 June 1944	Birth of Anne-Marie Claverie, Pierre's only sibling
1949	Pierre joins the *Saint-Do*, a Dominican-run scout troop
1 November 1954	Start of the Algerian War of Independence
June 1956	Pierre sits baccalauréat C, specialising in mathematics, at Lycée Bugeaud, Algiers
September 1956	Pierre starts third level preparatory course in mathematics, chemistry and physics in Algiers
1 November 1957	Transfers to Grenoble University to continue studying mathematics, chemistry and physics
7 December 1958	Clothed as a Dominican novice in Lille

8 December 1959	Simple profession
June 1962	Starts 16 months of military service in Algiers as an air force assistant chaplain
5 July 1962	Algeria gains its independence
1 November 1964	Solemn profession
4 July 1965	Ordination to the priesthood at Le Saulchoir, the Dominican House of Studies near Paris
5 July 1967	Returns to Algeria to serve a rapidly declining Church and a newly independent country
November 1970	Theological adviser for one year to Mgr Scotto, Bishop of Constantine and Hippone
January 1973	Appointed Director of *Les Glycines*, the pastoral and study centre for the Archdiocese of Algiers
2 October 1981	Ordained Bishop of Oran
26 December 1991	Islamist party (Islamic Salvation Front) gains a resounding victory in the first round of the legislative elections
11 January 1992	Second round of elections cancelled by the military-backed regime, unleashing a bitter 10-year civil war
8 May 1994	Assassination of Br Henri Vergès and Sr Paul-Hélène Saint-Raymond, the first of the 19 religious to be killed, the final one being Pierre

26/27 March 1996	Kidnapping of seven Trappists monks at Tibhirine, 96 km south of Algiers
21 May 1996	Announcement by Islamists of the execution of the seven Trappist monks
1 August 1996	Assassination of Pierre in Oran with his young friend and helper, Mohamed Bouchikhi
8 December 2018	Beatified in Oran, Algeria, along with 18 other martyred priests and religious (1994-1996)

....

Foreword

Timothy Radcliffe OP

FR MARTIN McGEE'S book on Blessed Pierre Claverie is a gift
for our time. Pierre's drama was lived out in a hot North African country a thousand miles to the south of Britain, but it is our
drama too. The questions that he faced then, we face today: How
to live with strangers? How to open our minds and hearts to people
with beliefs which are different to our own? How to make faithful
friendships?

I got to know Pierre long before I met him. My fellow Dominican student in Paris, Jean-Jacques Pérennès OP, worked with Pierre
in Algeria for ten years before he came to live with me in Rome, in
charge of the development of the Order's apostolate. Pierre always
stayed with us in Santa Sabina when he came to Rome, and we became friends too.

When the monks of Tibhirine were martyred, Jean-Jacques and I
decided that we must immediately go to Algeria to see our brethren.
They needed to be assured that they would be supported whether
they decided to stay in Algeria, with its growing violence, or leave.
All of them decided to stay.

We stayed in Pierre's simple and beautiful house in Oran where
he was bishop. It was he who taught me that dialogue is a way of
preaching the gospel. It in no way reduces discussion of faith to rel-

ativism. Jesus was a man of conversation. He was unafraid of engaging with anyone he met, whether the woman at the well in Samaria, prostitutes or rich Pharisees. Conversation leads to conversion, and Pierre showed us that in a good conversation, everyone is converted.

He took us around the diocese. The terrorists were disguising themselves as members of the security forces and setting up barricades, trying to catch the people whom they wanted, such as Pierre. So every morning he phoned his friends to see which areas were safer. The Church maintained libraries which Muslim university students could use. After the murder of one of the sisters who was a librarian, Pierre told us as we drove that he found it hard to keep his own diocesan library open. An old friar, Jean-Pierre Voreux OP, sitting in the back of the car, immediately volunteered: 'I am old enough to die. I will go to the library.' It was clear to us at the end of our stay that it was unlikely that Pierre would live for long.

A few weeks later I was in my study in Rome about to leave with Jean-Jacques to launch the new International Dominican Youth Movement in Spain. Just as we were leaving for the airport, the phone rang and we learnt of Pierre's murder and of that of his friend and helper, Mohamed Bouchikhi. We flew to Spain and as soon as possible I made my way to Oran for the funeral. When I arrived, I found a sister still collecting the remains of Pierre and Mohamed with a teaspoon.

The cathedral was filled with Christians and Muslims, their presence together a fruit of his gift for friendship. At the end some of us were invited to give our testimonies to Pierre and what he had meant to us. I remember a young woman who had drifted from Islam and become an atheist. She stood up and said that because of Pierre, she had returned to her Muslim faith and that he was a bishop for the Muslims too. Then the cathedral was filled with a quiet sound, as the Muslims murmured, 'He was our bishop too.' The three subsequent times that I have returned to Algeria since then, I have always found the tomb of Pierre covered with flowers left by Christians and Muslims, flowers in the desert.

The beatification of Pierre and his 18 companions on 8 December 2018 was a sort of miraculous moment. There were barricades again, but this time to protect the friends and relatives of the martyrs. More than 100 Muslim leaders, civil and religious, attended the ceremony and were thunderously applauded by the congregation. That evening we watched a performance of the play *Pierre & Mohamed*, written by a young French Dominican, Adrien Candiard OP, which explores their friendship. The play was attended by Mohamed's mother, who blew a kiss to the actor playing her son, and hugged the bishop.

As far as I know, this is the first time that the government of a Muslim-majority country gave such an enthusiastic welcome to the Christian celebration of our martyrs. How is this possible? It is because Pierre and the other religious gave their lives to the Algerian people and shared their suffering. The first martyrs were Sister Paul-Hélène Saint-Raymond, a Little Sister of the Assumption, and a Marist Brother Henri Vergès, who were murdered in May 1994. When Archbishop Henri Teissier warned his priests and religious of the danger of staying, Sister Paul-Hélène said, 'Father, our lives are already given away.' They could not be taken.

Christianity centres on the Eucharist, the gift of Christ's body. How can we celebrate that without trying to become ourselves gifts and learning to receive the other as a gift too? Pierre said : 'Giving one's life for this reconciliation [between Muslims and Christians], as Jesus gave his life in order to tear down the wall of hatred that separated Jews, Greeks, pagans, slaves, free persons – isn't this a way of celebrating the sacrifice of Jesus?'[1]

Few of us in the West are ever likely to respond with the full gift of our life as martyrs. But Pierre believed that we all are summoned to what he called white martyrdom: 'White martyrdom is what one strives to live each day, the giving of one's life drop by drop – in a look, in being present, in a smile, a gesture of concern, a service, in all of those things that makes one's life a life that is shared, given, bestowed upon others. This is where openness and detachment take on the meaning of martyrdom, of immolation – in letting go of life.'[2] That is our vocation, to become a gift. If we do so, what wonderful things may happen?

·················
Preface

THE BEATIFICATION of Bishop Pierre Claverie OP, and his 18 companion martyrs (1994-1996), took place in the Basilica of Santa Cruz, Oran, Algeria on 8 December 2018. This, the first be-atification to be celebrated in an overwhelmingly Muslim country, was held in the presence of the Algerian minister for religious affairs, Mohamed Aïssa, the local governor and numerous imams and Muslim friends of the small Christian community. It was fitting that there should be such a strong Muslim presence as the many Muslims (an estimated 150,000–200,000) who had lost their lives in the civil war (1992-2002) were also remembered in the service. Among the slain were 114 imams, assassinated for refusing to condone violence.

In his message to the congregation Pope Francis declared: 'Through the Beatification of our nineteen brothers and sisters, the Church wishes to bear witness to her desire to continue working for dialogue, harmony and friendship. We believe that this unprecedented event in your country will trace in the Algerian sky a great sign of fraternity addressed to the entire world.'[1] This fraternity was something for which Blessed Pierre Claverie had knowingly and willingly given his life. He wished above all to be Jesus' reconciling presence in places of suffering and distress, what he called the 'fault lines' of a broken humanity.

The Certainty of Being Loved is perhaps best described as a spiritual biography. It traces the spiritual journey of Pierre Claverie, born in 1938 in Bab el Oued, Algiers, the fourth generation of a family of European settlers. As a young man he experienced the anguish of the Algerian war of independence (1954-1962), and later the bitterness of the Algerian civil war (1992-2002). Growing up in Algiers, Pierre was totally unaware of his Muslim neighbours who made up 90 per cent of the population. In his own words he lived 'in a colonial bubble'. His realization, upon joining the Dominicans in France, that he had been blind to the plight and suffering of the Algerian people came as a great shock and spiritual awakening. This 'conversion' experience would eventually lead Pierre to offer his life as a ransom for peace and reconciliation between Christians and Muslims.

At the age of 11 Pierre joined the Scout Troop, St Jacques, run by the Dominicans friars in Algiers. As a result of his close relationship with the friars his faith blossomed and his leadership potential also found an outlet. In 1957 Pierre set out for France to study science at the University of Grenoble. On completion of his first year of study he decided to join the Dominican novitiate in Lille. The charism of St Dominic is expressed through a community life of prayer, study and preaching, a lifestyle which suited Pierre's outgoing personality and natural gifts. In the novitiate he discovered silent prayer which he practiced assiduously for the rest of his life. He wrote excitedly to his parents that he was convinced that this discovery would become 'the happiness of my life.'[2] As a friar, priest and bishop he led a very active life but all of this activity was founded on an intense life of prayer and reflection. He was conscious that all of his undertakings would bear no lasting fruit unless they were rooted in an intimate relationship with the Risen Lord and his indwelling Spirit.

Pierre was to remain in France, apart from a period of military service in Algeria, until 1967. On his return to an independent Algeria he found a decimated Catholic community struggling to support the fledgling state in its social projects. When he was appointed

Bishop of Oran in 1981 Islamic fundamentalism had begun to flourish and tougher times lay ahead for Pierre and the tiny Christian community. It was in such a climate of tension and violence that Pierre lived out his ideal of Christian holiness.

In Pierre's reflections and retreat talks we can clearly see his understanding of the spiritual life. He wrote frequently in the diocesan magazine *Le Lien* (The Link) about holiness and what it entails. The paschal mystery, Christ's saving passion, death and resurrection, was at the heart of Pierre's understanding of Christianity. He never tired of reminding people that every time they left the self behind in order to serve others they were becoming more Christ-like. In his own words: 'I was dead, I love, I resurrect, I live anew. Thus each time in my life that I lose myself a little, love, leave myself behind a little, I renew within myself the life of Jesus Christ: each time Jesus Christ will be born in me and the resurrection of Jesus will do its work in me.'[3]

In 1993 Pierre and his companion martyrs had been put under sentence of death by the Armed Islamic Group (GIA) who had given all foreigners an ultimatum to leave Algeria by 1 December or face execution. All of the 19 martyrs chose to remain in Algeria out of a love of Christ and a desire to serve the Muslim people. As Pierre wrote towards the end of his life: 'I have worked tirelessly for dialogue and friendship among peoples, cultures and religions. All of that has probably merited for me death and I am willing to run the risk.'[4]

Pierre was a man of dialogue who sought to value difference and to learn from it. His lifelong struggle for peace and reconciliation between Christians and Muslims speaks strongly to our tormented times. Pierre's witness, his martyrdom, reminds us that the light can overcome the darkness. As he wrote in an editorial in the diocesan magazine in 1982: 'The saints, all the saints, are our living Gospel, written in letters of flesh and blood: on the obscure chaos of a humanity searching for light, they proclaim the greatness of God and

The Certainty of Being Loved

the greatness of humanity, because 'man is the human face of God' (Gregory of Nyssa).'[5]

Part 1

....

*Escaping from
the Colonial Bubble*

The Claverie family, 8 December 1946

1

A Colonial Background

ON COMING to realise the nature of the 'colonial bubble' in which he had grown up in Algiers Pierre's initial reaction was one of bitterness: 'I lived my childhood in Algiers, in a working class district of this cosmopolitan, Mediterranean city. Unlike other Europeans born in the country or the small towns, I never had any Arab friends, neither in my local school in which they were absent, nor at the lycée where there were very few of them and where the Algerian war had begun to create an explosive atmosphere. We weren't racist, only indifferent, ignoring the majority of this country's inhabitants. They were a part of the background to our outings, of the décor to our encounters and our lives. They were never partners. And nevertheless we were Christians ...' [1]

It was in his early twenties, while studying in France, that the full significance of his colonial existence, his life in 'the colonial bubble', became devastatingly clear to Pierre. He had lived a life unaware of his Arab neighbours, totally oblivious to their inferior status and suffering. And the local Christian community had done nothing to awaken his conscience to their plight. This was the beginning of his vocation to the religious life and the priesthood, a vocation which would be dedicated to undoing this wrong. And this 'conversion experience' is the key to understanding Pierre's subsequent decisions and steadfastness in the face of many trials and much suffering.

AN UNCONSCIOUS RACISM

Modern-day Algeria has experienced seven large-scale invasions: the first invasion, in 1100 BC, was carried out by the Phoenicians-Carthaginians and the final one took place in 1830 when the French forces landed at Sidi-Ferruch.[2] This new colonial presence, made up of European settlers from France, Spain, Italy and Malta, laid claim by force to the country. Pierre was a fourth generation *pied-noir*, or European settler, brought up in Bab el Oued, a working class district of Algiers. For Pierre and his family Algeria was their home although the family did retain links with France, going on holidays there every other year.

In her book *Des Européennes en situation coloniale: Algérie 1830-1939*[3] Claudine Robert-Guiard notes that the *pieds-noirs* were not conscious of showing racist attitudes towards the Arabs, and often refused to accept that this was the case. She writes: 'Racism towards Arabs is more often than not denied by the *Pieds-noirs*, not so much, it would seem, by a conscious refusal to recognise a disagreeable reality as by the impossibility of seeing this reality.'[4] She gives the example of Fr Bérenguer who supported the Algerian war of independence and remained on in Algeria after independence until his death. In a series of interviews about his life he recounts that in his village of Lourmel in the Oran region he had never witnessed even the slightest racism by the French or the Spanish towards Arabs whereas he had witnessed anti-Semitism.

Claudine Robert-Guiard doesn't doubt that Fr Bérenguer is telling the truth from his perspective. She explains his blindness as follows: 'The Muslims didn't have citizenship rights and during the inter-war years they didn't pose a threat to European interests, thus racism towards them showed itself under the form of paternalism or a contemptuous air-brushing of them out of the picture. The Arabs were part of the scenery (*décor*) in which Europeans had set themselves up, mere silhouettes, visible or invisible according to circumstances. Without there being any organised segregation, they were kept apart from the European social sphere.'[5]

It was likewise with Étienne Claverie, Pierre's father: 'I confess that at no time in my life did I have an understanding of my mission as a true Christian in the place where I lived in complete indifference to the other community which nevertheless engulfed us. I understood too late, and how grateful I would be if the *pied-noir* community [now living in exile in France] could come to the same understanding.'[6]

A COLONIAL LEGACY

The two communities lived side by side but, apart from economic necessities, had practically no social contact. There were often good neighbourly relations, especially outside the cities, but friendship across the social boundaries was rare, understandably so as the *pieds-noirs* did not regard the Algerians as their equals. For the most part they were convinced that they had a 'civilising mission' to accomplish, namely, to bring the benefits of a Christian and Western civilization to the Muslim world.

It was into this closed world that Pierre and the well-known author Marie Cardinal were born. Marie Cardinal's family owned a large farm and, unlike Pierre, she spoke Arabic as a child and spent a lot of her time when she was young in the company of her father's farm workers. She had a great affection for them and she had, from an early age, supported the struggle for Algerian independence.

She well understood the colonial mentality: 'A coloniser is a person who goes into exile in a foreign land for the benefit of his country and his own benefit. It is not a gratuitous act. He works hard and makes use of his national ideal like a cudgel. The coloniser wishes to enrich himself at the best price and he does so without shame because he is sure of the rightness of his cause since he is superior. His morality is the best, his lifestyle is the best, his social morality is the best, his systems and his laws are the best, his religion is the best. By imposing all this he is doing good. He is certain of this; there is no bad faith on his part. When he doubts, it is not about himself and all that he represents. It is about the method which he has used to impose himself.'[7]

To understand the challenge which Pierre faced in coming to terms with his colonial past, a past which isolated him totally from the majority population, one needs to have some insight into the colonial set-up. According to a law enacted in 1865, 35 years after the French invasion of Algeria, all Algerian Muslims became French subjects but not French citizens. Because settlers and Muslims had separate legal systems, Algerians didn't have the right to vote unless they made an individual request to the Council of State and gave up their right to be judged according to Islamic law, the *Shari'a*. Understandably, very few Muslims were willing to do this as it was tantamount to apostasy: 'As a result, by 1936, after seventy-five years of "assimilation", no more than 2,500 Muslims had actually crossed the bar to French citizenship.'[8] Alistair Horne goes on to state that 'as late as 1956 – two years after the Algerian war had broken out – Governor-General Lacoste admitted that no more than eight out of 864 higher administrative posts were held by Muslims.'[9]

In addition to these voting inequalities, there were also huge socio-economic differences, especially with regards to education. Benjamin Stora tells us that in 1945 out of 1,250,000 Algerian children only 100,000 were attending primary school whereas all of the settlers' children were doing so. Likewise, in the University of Algiers in 1945 there were 4,500 students, of whom only 150 were Muslims or 3.3%.[10] These stark statistics tell their own story of segregation and discrimination, a repressive structure of governance which would inevitably lead to an explosion of violence.

THE SÉTIF MASSACRE

A key event which sealed the fate of French rule in Algeria was the Sétif massacre. On May 8, 1945, a VE day parade was organized in the town of Sétif. However, the majority of the Muslim inhabitants were in no mood to celebrate the Allied victory. After two years of poor harvests, wartime austerities and no rainfall since the previous January, the local people were ripe for revolt. They wished to have a share in the freedom being celebrated by the VE day parades throughout France and elsewhere. According to Alistair Horne: 'On walls graffiti appeared overnight exhorting: "Muslims awaken!" "It's the Muslim flag that will float over North Africa!" Or, with a more direct menace: "Français, you will be massacred by the Muslims!" ' [11]

What exactly happened during the parade is disputed. The parade led by the Muslim scouts had banners with slogans such as: 'We want to be your equals', '*Istiqlal*' (Independence) and 'Algeria for the Arabs'.[12] Some of the Muslim banners calling for Algerian independence were seized; shots were fired and a number of Europeans were killed. The gendarmes in their turn killed some of the Muslim marchers. The rebellion spread to the surrounding countryside with some of the European farmers being killed. In all, 103 Europeans lost their lives during this period of unrest. The French retaliated massively in Sétif, Guelma and Kerrata. Inaccessible Muslim villages were strafed from the air, two naval vessels bombarded other villages. Estimates of the Muslim causalities vary from 1,020 to 45,000, with the French General Tubert, in his report on the massacre, giving an estimate of 15,000.[13]

The reaction of the 132,000 Algerian soldiers who had fought on the Allied side during the war can only be imagined. Was this the freedom for which they had risked their lives? One of them happened to be Sergeant Ben Bella, who in 1962 became the first president of an independent Algeria. He wrote: ' The horrors of the Constantine area [where Sétif lies] in 1945 succeeded in persuading me of the only path; Algeria for the Algerians.'[14] The point of no return in Franco-Algerian relations had been reached. The renowned Algerian writer in French, Kateb Yacine, had taken part, as a 15-year-old schoolboy, in this protest march in Sétif. For him it was the moment when the scales fell from his eyes: 'One could call that [Sétif] lost illusions. We ourselves had lost the illusion that we could have independence, just like that, bestowed from on high, like a gift from the French leftists. As for the colonialists they also had come to the end of an illusion because they thought that, thanks to this great massacre, they would have peace for ten years, but what kind of peace?'[15] These indiscriminate reprisals had effectively destroyed all hope of a peaceful co-existence on equal terms between the *pieds-noirs* and the Algerians.[16]

In the light of the Sétif débâcle, the French government passed a bill in 1947 creating an elected Assemblée Algérienne with two electoral colleges, each containing 60 members. The first was to represent the *pieds-noirs* and the 60,000 Muslims who had educational qualifications or a record of service to the state. The second college would represent the remaining nine million indigenous Algerians. However, when elections were held in 1948, the French administration indulged in blatant electoral fraud to ensure that the majority of the elected Muslim candidates would be favourable to the government. Inevitably, this injustice only made Algerian nationalists more determined in their opposition to French rule.[17]

THE OPPOSITE OF LOVE

The total breakdown of relationships between the *pieds-noirs* and the Algerian people came to a head during the war of independence. The *pieds-noirs* were blind to the necessity for a generous accommodation which would acknowledge Algeria's right to independence. Blinded by fear and a superiority complex, they destroyed any possibility of a peaceful settlement. To read Mouloud Feraoun's diary allows one to appreciate the merciless terror of the war years (1954-1962) and its traumatic impact on the Algerian people. Mouloud, a Kabyle, was a distinguished writer in French, a primary school teacher, subsequently a school inspector, and a person who refused to engage in violence of any kind. (A Kabyle is a member of the Berber people living in the mountainous coastal area east of Algiers who speak Berber and who were, and are, more open to Christianity than the Arab Muslims.) His *Journal 1955-1962* [18] is a searing indictment of violence on both sides, but in particular of the complete abandonment of moral values by the French army in its desperate bid to pacify the local population.

Mouloud recounts a long litany of heartless intimidation, pillage, rape, arbitrary arrest and summary executions as the French army vainly tried to terrorise the unfortunate Kabyles into submission; many of them were also being intimidated, and killed on a whim by the local National Liberation Front, *Front de Libération Nationale*. This was a bloody and ruthless attempt by a colonial power, and the *pieds-noirs*, to hold on to power and privilege, largely abandoning in the process any sense of natural justice and morality.

In a lengthy reflection in his journal in December 1955 Mouloud seeks to answer the question: Why have Algerians, even the least well off, been willing to sacrifice everything in order to achieve independence? What about the 'marriage' between France and Algeria? Mouloud scornfully replies:

> The truth is that there never was a marriage. No. The French have remained apart. Disdainfully apart. The French have remained foreigners. They believed that they were Algeria. Now that we consider ourselves to be fairly strong or that we believe them to be somewhat weak, we say to them: no, gentlemen, we are Algeria. You are foreigners in our land.
>
> What would have been needed for us to love each other? To know each other first of all; well, we do not know each other.

If you ask a Kabyle woman what it means to be a French man, she will say that he is an infidel, a man who is often handsome and strong but pitiless. He is perhaps intelligent. His intelligence comes from the demon as does his strength. What does she expect from a French man, nothing good. Neither his justice, sharp as a sword, nor his charity which is accompanied by insults and jostling. What is a native for a European? He is a man of sorrow, the domestic help. A bizarre creature with a ridiculous life style, a distinctive costume, an impossible language. A more or less dirty individual, more or less ragged, more or less antipathetic. In any case a being apart, well apart, who should be left to his own devices. These are commonplaces that are almost childish to recall in such a summary manner. But this is the source of the evil. There is no need to search elsewhere. For a century we rubbed shoulders without curiosity; it only remains to harvest this conscious indifference which is the opposite of love.[19]

'I AM NOT VERY PROUD OF MY BEHAVIOUR'

Pierre's family weren't consciously racist but they were indifferent to the surrounding Muslim religion and culture. In a searingly honest letter to his parents in November 1960 Pierre wrote: 'We the Claveries did nothing ... to inform ourselves about the real situation of the Arabs.'[20] In response to Pierre's growing enthusiasm for the Arab culture and language, Étienne, Pierre's father, made a frank and humble admission (letter of July 31, 1968) of his own indifference in the past to the native culture. Now, when it was too late, he expressed his regrets: 'So you see, indeed now that it's too late I've got regrets about having rubbed shoulders [with the Arab world] for so long without, to a certain extent, having noticed its existence, without having the least curiosity about understanding it, even less about penetrating it. So much so that even now I don't grasp any of

its reactions and cannot rid myself of an instinctive mistrust of it....
Moreover, I am not very proud of my behaviour and I hope that you
can bring to our homeland brothers, what now, too late, I realise I
could, perhaps, have given them.'[21]

In later life Pierre felt angry and upset that he could never recall hearing anyone preach in church that the Arabs were also their
neighbours and were to be loved too: 'Not to recognise the other
side, to pass by without seeing, to live in bubbles, all of that exposes
us to explosions of endless violence. I had to cope with the consequences: to try to come out of my bubbles (colonial but also cultural
and religious ...), to fight against everything which imprisons and
crushes, to open the windows (of the heart and the mind), to pull
down the walls which separate ...'[22]

It's easy for us, says Pierre, to relate to those who are like us, who
belong to the same tribe. However, those who are different, for example, those who have a different culture or religion, these people
can threaten us. That was exactly what happened to the Algerian
Church in colonial times, according to Pierre. The Algerian was
recognised only in so far as he became part of their landscape, and
entered into their system of values: 'And those who were different,
namely nine-tenths of the world that surrounded us, were ignored,
rejected or devalued by a little mockery. All these traditions were
strange ... And we thought that happily they would soon change
thanks to our beneficial influence'.[23]

THE CONSEQUENCES OF STRUCTURAL SIN

Growing up in Algeria the only Algerians whom he came to know
were at the lycée, and these few students had been completely assimilated to the French way of life. It was only when Pierre joined
the Dominicans in France [24] that he came fully to realise that he had
shut out of his existence all those people, all of those neighbours
to whom the parable of the Good Samaritan draws our attention.

The European settlers' unconscious fear of the Algerian other had blinded them to their existence. The same phenomenon, comments Pierre, can also be seen in inter–personal relationships. We can ignore the person next to us because they are different and we fear this difference. The person thus ignored will eventually become aggressive because they 'have a need of recognition and they will make their presence felt by force.' [25]

Pierre, in one of his retreat talks, comments that words can take on many meanings depending on the circumstances, something we need to be aware of. Thus in his own life as an Algerian *pied-noir* he went to Church and heard many sermons on love of God and love of neighbour: 'No one ever told us that the Algerians were also [as well as the Christians of European origin] our neighbours! Never! They were the others, they were part of the landscape. The neighbour was my *own* neighbour. There were poor people, but they were poor Christians. There were people who specialised in Algerians; this was the work of the White Fathers and Sisters. I'm caricaturing things and giving my own account; others had a different experience; but I note that I lived my childhood without ever really meeting a single Algerian; to meet, yes in the streets, passing them by without seeing them. We were not bad, nor mean; we were also Christians. For me that's awful.' [26]

The price paid for this collective isolation from the Algerian population was high; it led to the massive departure of the *pieds-noirs* immediately after independence. This, in Pierre's eyes, was the result of a collective sin. Although no one could be held individually responsible, everyone bore the consequences of this structural sin. All their best acts were in some way tainted by being part of this collectivity. Even many of the most generous acts by the *pieds-noirs* were interpreted as being another way of keeping the native population in subjection.

It was this realisation which impelled Pierre to return to an independent Algeria in order to live a counter-witness of openness to difference and to the value of diversity, what he calls elsewhere 'a plural humanity'. And in this way he hoped that he would be able to help the Algerian people not to repeat the same mistake as the *pieds-noirs*: to become closed in on themselves, oblivious to the riches which difference can bring.

A VOCATION TO BREAK DOWN BARRIERS

It was into this colonial world that Pierre Claverie was born. His failure, when growing up, to notice his Arab neighbours came to haunt him and to radically change his life. He says that his escape from the 'colonial bubble' and the colonial myth of superiority was the beginning of his religious vocation, a vocation to break down barriers and to see every person as of equal dignity and value. In the aftermath of the savage war of independence Pierre returned to his native country and attempted to make some amends for a colonial past (and his unwitting participation in it) which had deeply scarred the Algerian psyche and which still, more than 50 years on, makes relationships between Algeria and France tense and problematic.

In the aftermath of Algerian independence Pierre wrote a very poignant letter to his parents as they prepared to leave Algeria for good and go into exile in France. He fully appreciated the pain which this uprooting would cause them as they had known no other existence apart from their life in Algeria: 'Poor little house as papa said in one of his last epistles. Of course we will no longer see the panorama from Notre- Dame d'Afrique to the sea, of course we will no longer take the windswept walk along rue Koechlin – and all those images will become part of a store of memories.'

He goes on to say that these memories and places are not what ultimately matter but the human relationships and friendships which they have formed and which will remain, no matter where they live: 'You are not without roots. You are not homeless because our roots are in people's hearts (and not in the land or bricks) and you will find again all those friends where you are going.' He reassures them that they have been faithful to their mission in life, namely, to be good parents. The Algerian war and its tragic consequences were beyond their understanding and overwhelmed them: '*The family goes on, continues to spread its peace and its spirit of union. In its own way it wages a battle, it conquers territories and from these no one can dislodge it.*' As for himself, he is free to become one of those pioneers who will set about rebuilding Algeria, one of those who 'have nothing to lose and who have consecrated their lives to the service of others.' [27]

2

A United Family

WHEN HIS SISTER Anne-Marie spoke at Pierre's funeral her words were concise and packed with meaning, honesty and love: 'He had the privilege, like me too, to be born of parents for whom the word "love" wasn't an empty word. The love which they bore each other and which they had for us was exceptional: in its discretion, its abnegation but also in its extraordinary depth. I believe that it is out of that love that my brother's faith was born. In addition, he had inherited from our mother her *joie de vivre* and her great goodness, and from our father the ability to reflect, and the precision of his thinking. And, then, all that he possessed, he wished to share, to give away.'[1]

Pierre, born on May 8, 1938 to Étienne Claverie and Louise Maillard, lived at 4 rue Koechlin in Bab el Oeud, a lively and vibrant working class neighbourhood of Algiers. In 1944 Anne-Marie, his only sibling, was born. Pierre went to the local state primary school in the nearby rue Rochambeau. Here he was surrounded exclusively by *pieds-noirs* classmates, the children of the European settlers with family roots in France, Spain, Italy, Portugal and Malta. The native Algerians lived in the Kasbah and in the outskirts of the city. Thus it was that Pierre had no Algerian friends at primary school. It was much the same story when he progressed to the prestigious Lycée Bugeaud where he passed with honours (*avec mention*) his baccalauréat C, which specialised in mathematics. Although this establishment had a few Algerian students, Pierre never got to make friends with any of them. In fact, the only Algerian whom he knew well as a child and adolescent was the family's housekeeper who was very devoted to him.

Pierre was fortunate to be brought up in a family which helped him discover, in the ordinary events of everyday life, a God of love. He writes: 'I owe to my happy childhood the image of a God who is close, attentive, respectful of my freedom, whose love leads one to be good to others. I truly believe that I was able to discover and experience from a young age – thanks to my parents and my environment – the liberating power of a trust given and received. The humanity of God, as shown by Jesus in the gestures and words of a simple, everyday existence, marked me lastingly.'[2]

The Claverie family were a very tightly knit unit; everything concerning the life of their children was of interest to their parents, and *vice versa*. Étienne would write to Pierre when he was a priest in Algeria: 'We spend the better part of our life waiting for something which comes from you or has reference to you.'[3] Both parents had difficult childhoods with Louise losing her mother at the age of 14 and Étienne being born outside wedlock when his mother was 16 years old. He saw his father on only one occasion when he was a little boy. Their difficult childhoods made both parents determined that their own children should experience something different, a stability and security which they themselves had lacked. Pierre's father spent his whole working life as an executive with the Shell Company in Algiers, ending up as head of public relations. He had been offered the post of Director of Shell Senegal but refused this promotion because he wished to remain in Algiers.[4]

Writing to his parents in May 1972 for mother's day, Pierre states clearly his indebtedness to the unconditional love of his family, a love which gave him a strong sense of his own self-identity and an uncommon self-confidence and personal security: 'I often think about you all and say to myself how lucky we were to have, at the wellspring of our life, this extraordinary equilibrium which the certainty of being loved gives, without fuss. I believe that one finds there the strength to subsequently travel along any path however difficult it may be.' [5]

In another letter to his parents in December 1972 he returns to the same theme and expresses his gratitude for having been brought up in a loving family: 'We have, all of us, the extraordinary grace of having discovered that we existed for each other and that that didn't make us prisoners of each other, but contributed, on the contrary, to freeing us interiorly so that we could give ourselves better to others.' [6] His parents had transmitted God's selfless love to Pierre and his sister, and this had freed them, in their turn, to go out and love others selflessly. And this family love was the rock which enabled Pierre to hold firm in good times and bad.

I WAS ABLE TO PERCEIVE A LIGHT

Both of his parents grew up rather lukewarm Catholics with the Church providing a cultural backdrop to their lives. This all changed when Pierre, at the age of 11, joined the scout troop, known as the *Saint-Do*, which was run by the Dominicans friars in Algiers. From then on he was immersed in the life of the Church. His father decided to accompany his son on his faith journey and gradually the Christian faith became a deep and important part of his life too. We can see this clearly in his letters. Not only can Étienne, and his mother Louise, follow with interest Pierre's Sunday homilies on Radio Alger, but Étienne can also enter into dialogue with him about developments in Church practice and thinking in the wake of Vatican II. Étienne had a deep grasp of the core of the Christian faith, namely that it is first and foremost about our relationship with Christ and secondly about sharing the fruits of this friendship with others.

His letter to Pierre's novice master in November 1958 reveals a person of profound faith and spirituality, a man who is close to

Christ and trusts in him: 'Last Thursday's plane took our son Pierre towards his new destiny ... Now that divine Providence has brought about everything according to his will, it is time to introduce our-selves to you and to help you to get to know Pierre better through his parents.' He goes on to say that religion was only a formality for him until Pierre began going to catechism classes and that nothing, or very little, in their family background would have predisposed Pierre towards a priestly vocation. For Étienne this shows that his calling comes from God.

> To his [Pierre's] great joy I began to accompany him to church. I began, in order to be a 'worthwhile discussion partner' for him, to get ready for mass using a superb daily missal which he, in league with his sister, had given me. And it's thus that little by little I was able to perceive a Light, to better under-stand and follow my son's development. My Faith is still very weak and uncertain but I know that the Lord, who ceaselessly shows me his care, will allow me to be more closely united to Him through my son, his future Servant. His mother feels the same way, she whom I always tell my children is the natu-ral link who unites them to God ... Our son is now yours. You have all our prayers. Once again may he delight you as he has always delighted us. He is a good and loyal youngster...[7]

Étienne Claverie, for someone who had no theological formation or serious Christian upbringing, showed a remarkable ability to understand the theology of the Second Vatican Council. One Sunday morning in 1969 he was watching a TV programme featuring the great French theologian Yves Congar OP who was talking about authority and freedom in the Church. Étienne was surprised and thrilled to hear Fr Congar express his own ideas: 'I am always flabbergasted to hear my own thinking expressed on topics where in fact I have had no formation. It is really very strange and thrilling. Maman is just as flabbergasted to hear what I've been telling her all year long.'[8] In his letter to Pierre's novice master we can see this same remarkable spiritual insight and intuition at work.

Étienne believed strongly in the divine Providence which guided his daily life. Provided a person does their best to have an informed conscience, he believed that they could be at peace. One shouldn't seek to complicate too much the Christian way of life: 'Everything that God does and wishes is very simple, of a supernatural simplicity, and I hold that it is a sin [seeking to complicate things] – with which the Church is stained whether it likes it or not – which clouds our vision. If God is impenetrable to us, Christ has explained the designs of his Father. To listen to him should be sufficient.'[9]

In the midst of the post-Conciliar confusion and disagreements in the Church Étienne comments: 'No reason to be in disarray and to lose one's footing as long as we're allowed to love in the shadow of the Cross. Trust should be one of the chief virtues of Christ's disciples. Trust in love and in his charity. Different versions of the Mass and anti-establishment motions, they will all be blown away by the wind. Born in controversy, His Church will often experience this again. But His Word is eternal and the devil is powerless before the one who listens to it.'[10]

THE GIFT OF SELFLESS LOVE

In March 1969 Pierre shared his reflections with his parents about their lack of family roots, something which he viewed, on the whole, positively. They hadn't got a family history to uphold or defend which gave them a sense of detachment: 'As for us we haven't any right to claim from anyone: our only riches are to try to live together, loving one another, for the little time which has been given us. The rest doesn't belong to us, neither past nor future. I find that to be a very exceptional grace for which we are also indebted to "Providence".'[11] One could argue, of course, that this sense of detachment could cut them off from others and from the wider community. In fact, the Claverie family managed to reach out to the wider community through the local Church and Étienne had his work contacts and family friends. However, the family unit was the core of their existence and it was there that Pierre and his sister, Anne-Marie, found their inner stability and equilibrium.

Pierre's sense of being part of a closely knit family can be seen in his frequent letters to his parents. On his departure for France as a 19-year-old Pierre started writing regular letters to his parents in Algeria. During his first month he wrote a total of 10! After that he settled down to a weekly letter, usually written on a Sunday. His father, Étienne, carefully filed these. Over 2,000 letters were written between 1957 and 1996 and they are now in the care of Pierre's sister and brother-in-law.[12] Those letters written while he was a Dominican friar and priest in Algiers frequently contained requests to his mother for various personal items such as shoes, jumpers, shirts, trousers. He comments that all these items are very expensive in Algiers and, on account of their poor quality, only last a few weeks. He ends his shopping list by saying: 'There's no need for Maman to become alarmed; I'm far from being a tramp and I carefully look after what I've got: (The proof: I've just resewn the buttons on the back pocket of my trousers...).'[13] However, his request for items also includes jeans and two bottles of perfume (*Paco Rabane*) for his friends, a heater for the guard on duty at the nunciature and countless other requests every few months. While this shows his closeness to his parents, it could also be seen, perhaps, as taking his mother a little for granted. When I made this point in an e-mail to Pierre's sister, Anne-Marie, she didn't agree with my feeling of unease. She replied:

> I can understand your question and your 'malaise' because in the letters that were published, it is my father who is quoted. But my mother would always add a handwritten note in which she expressed her love for Pierre and her concerns about his

well-being. If my dad was dealing with the intellectual and spiritual aspect of these exchanges, our mother was dealing with the concrete and the material: she was a true '*mère poule*' [mother hen]. Her letters were short because her eyesight was not good as a result of a fall as a child from the seventh floor of a building where she lived in Algiers. She was called the miracle child! So, reading and writing were difficult for her. Our dad, who, you may know, had a glass eye (on account of a suicide attempt at the age of twenty), was also a '*mal-voyant*' [had impaired eyesight], but he couldn't imagine not being in close contact with his far-flung children who, with our mother, were at the center of his life.

Our mother was like a ray of sunshine, devoted to her husband and children, generous and open to others to a fault (when we were kids, we used to tease her and say that she was too good to people!). She was not 'soft': as a young woman she was a pioneer in the field of physical therapy, loved the outdoors (swimming, skiing).[14]

A HEALTHY VISION OF LOVE

In the three volumes of correspondence which have been published 85 percent of the letters addressed to Pierre are written by his father. As a result the reader comes to understand Étienne and his relationship with Pierre much better than Pierre's relationship with his mother. However, as Anne-Marie points out, his relationship with his mother was equally close, though inevitably of a different kind, given his parents' contrasting personalities. Anne-Marie comments: 'Pierre was the perfect combination of our father and mother. His openness to others, his '*joie de vivre*' came from our mother, his intellect from our father'.

As for the parental relationship itself, Anne-Marie comments in the same e-mail: 'My father adored my mother and always spoke to

us about her as the person who had saved his life. Having had himself a charming but unfaithful mother he was probably incredibly
happy to have a wonderful spouse and by extension a superb mother, which she was! Worthy of veneration? My brother and I had the
extraordinary good fortune of having been conceived by these two
beings!' [15]

Pierre's confidence and trust in his father and mother and his
experience of his parents' love were the bedrock of his personal
integration and stability. His father's selfless devotion to the well-
being of Pierre is especially striking in the field of Pierre's religious
development. Although at that time a lapsed Catholic, once Pierre
joined the scouts and became a practising Catholic, Étienne decided
that he should accompany him on his faith journey, to be, in his
own words a 'worthwhile discussion partner' for his son. This is a
wonderful example of a parent whose first priority is the wellbeing
of his children.

Étienne developed a strong relationship with Pierre but not an
overpowering one. Watching a TV programme where parents and
children were discussing their relationships, Étienne laments that
they are talking about the latest theories and fashions 'but no one
simply talks about love which is still more simply "the gift".' [16] On
starting his military service in 1962 Pierre was taken aback by the
coarseness and immaturity of some of his fellow soldiers. He wrote
to his mother: 'With daddy you gave me, unintentionally, but simply through your example, a solid affectivity, a true and healthy vision of love.' [17]

It was also this foundational family experience which gave Pierre
his deep appreciation of the centrality of relationships in human life
and all the more so in Christian living. In January 1972 he wrote to
his parents about his father's efforts on behalf of retired Shell em-
ployees: 'This [his father's efforts] strengthens my conviction that
it is not a matter of doing great things nor of moving heaven and
earth, but that life and happiness, on a daily basis, involve a lot of

little nothings which contribute to weaving a web of better relationships.'[18] Pierre himself had many intellectual gifts but he never allowed them to blind him to the priority of love, a gift received and nurtured in loving relationships, especially within the family circle. When preaching at the ordination Mass of his friend Jean-Jacques Pérennès OP in 1989, he remarked: 'His intellectual qualities haven't killed his humanity as is so often the case.'[19] Pierre knew, as a result of his family upbringing, that all the abstract theological ideas in the world won't save us if love is absent. Pierre was first and foremost a person in relationship.

TO LOVE PEOPLE JUST AS THEY ARE

Did Pierre's exceptionally strong family life and upbringing make him so secure that he didn't feel a need for the support of close friends? Jean-Jacques Pérennès OP comments that Pierre wasn't someone who wore his heart on his sleeve and wonders 'where were his struggles?'[20]

In his thorough and excellent biography, *Pierre Claverie Un Algérien par alliance* Jean-Jacques quotes a letter Pierre wrote to his parents in March 1959: 'I resemble in every respect my "brute" of a father; we have the same withdrawn disposition ... but if I don't talk more about my feelings it's not because they are lacking, I assure you.'[21]

Though Pierre may have had no confidant, he did undoubtedly have many good friends, people whom he accepted unconditionally and who in their turn loved him for who he was. His sister Anne-Marie describes his personality in terms which would suggest that he had all the qualities which attract friendship. She writes: 'He was very perceptive and generous although not afraid to call a spade a spade, yet always trying to find a solution to any problems which arose. Above all Pierre was joyful. He combined the sunny disposition of my mother with the thoughtful intelligence of my father, giving him a remarkable psychological balance. He seemed to have a great inner strength and was a confidant for many of his friends.'[22]

In March, 1973 Pierre wrote that he had paid a social visit to Hadj Zinaï, his dentist, with whom he had 'an excellent, very friendly conversation. I'm beginning to have real friends with whom I feel totally at ease and with whom I can talk at a very deep level.'[23] And on 19 April 1977 Pierre comments that he has been invited out by a young Moroccan couple, Mounir and Latifa, 'with whom I have struck up a real friendship.'[24] He also had a very good friendship with the Pakistani ambassador in Algiers, Mr Bukhari, with whom he frequently dined. And he had many other close Muslim friends especially in his almost 15 years as bishop in Oran. When he was installed as bishop on 9 October 1981 there weren't very many Algerians in the congregation whereas at his funeral the majority of the congregation were Muslims.

Among his closest friends was Redouane Rahal, a lawyer. They had known each other for over 24 years and during Pierre's time in Oran they saw each other on a daily basis. M. Rahal wrote that Pierre was 'a warm, fraternal and sincere friend' and that in speaking about him he felt 'as if he were almost speaking about himself so deep and strong was their friendship.'[25] Redouane also tells us that Pierre had good friends among the sheiks of the Muslim confraternities, such as Sheik Medhi Bouabdelli. These sheiks had remained faithful to the more open and tolerant form of Islam which had been the norm in Algeria until the 1970s.[26]

Pierre talks about friendship in a most profound manner in a letter to his parents in September 1967. He is talking about the challenge posed to the Claverie family by Eric, his future brother-in-law, the challenge to accept him for who he is with his American culture and all the differences which that implies: 'When one is 24/24 face to face with someone, one can ignore nothing of who they are and one has to accept them completely as they are and to love them just as they are and not for what they give us or for what we find of ourselves in them. There, that's when friendship begins to happen.'[27] Jean-Jacques comments:

> One knows in the end very little about Pierre Claverie. He doesn't appear to have had a confidant, to whom he opened his heart. His happy childhood and youth, his deep equilibrium, his 'faultless' progression appear to have preserved him from the floundering which is the common lot of many. Indeed there was the trial which he experienced following the disintegration of the Algeria he had known in his childhood, the leaving behind of what he called 'the colonial bubble'. This was for him a suffering which he never sought to hide and which those close to him witnessed discreetly. But then everything returned to normal, almost too much so, one might dare to say. One could just guess that responsibilities, sometimes, weighed upon him: all the time spent in reconciling people's sensitivities, managing the inevitable institutional heaviness. But that was already for him a way of giving his life away, another central theme in his spirituality.[28]

WE ARE REALLY VERY FRAGILE

Pierre enjoyed his community life and the companionship which it provided. Because he was a deeply integrated person who knew himself well and had a fulfilling prayer life, he doesn't appear to have had emotional crises. In a revealing comment to his parents in December 1967 about a fellow Dominican, who was requesting laicisation, Pierre wrote: 'We are really very fragile and if for one moment we lose our bearings and the meaning of what we're about, basically if we lose sight of the fact that we are here only for God and through Him, we risk stumbling on the least thing.'[29] Pierre had his sights fixed firmly on serving God and his relationship with the Lord appears to have been his main source of fulfilment.

I broached, by e-mail,[30] this question of friendship with some people who knew Pierre very well in Algeria. Mgr Teissier replied that Pierre was very close to his Dominican community in Algiers and especially Fr Voreux and he was also close to the parish team in El-Biar, Algiers, led by Fr Pierre Franz: 'But I believe that he shared most deeply with some of his friends from Oran like Maître[31] Nimour or Mr Bentchouk.' His sister Anne-Marie commented: 'That's right. Pierre did not confide easily. It's a family trait. He kept his confidences for my parents with whom he used to recharge his batteries as often as possible. Like him and my parents I don't know how to "tell my story". But I have a husband and children who can guess what I think and as for Pierre what he gave to others was enough to make him loved.'

In addition to his deep relationship with the Lord in prayer, his relationship with his parents was very open and loving. In his letters he confided in them and would have done this even more so on his visits home, as Anne-Marie states. In a letter in October 1962 to his wife, Louise, Étienne Claverie comments on his relationship with his son, who was also in Algiers doing his military service: 'And then our interminable conversations which go on very late into the night, talk which has come to support my view that our son and brother was, moreover, more and more my friend.'[32]

Above all, Pierre was a man of prayer. Any attempt to understand his life and witness will founder if this central reality of his life is not taken fully into account. Prayer, his relationship with God, was the place where Pierre found the strength to leave himself behind and to make space for others. Pierre wasn't lacking a confidant. He had found one both in his father and in the Lord.

3

A Time of Spiritual Awakening

WHEN preaching in June 1990 at the ordination of Br Philippe Cochinaux, Pierre could well have been describing his own religious awakening: 'To no longer have any need to impose oneself on others in order to win one's place in the sun, one's dignity in the eyes of others: to be able to exist in simplicity with the quiet assurance which the conviction of being loved gives, what a grace! Freed from oneself and ready to enter into a similar relationship with others: a source of inexhaustible life is to be found there. Nourished by this trusting relationship where parents, friends, religious brothers have a role, we are ready to hear God's call.' [1]

Joining the Dominican scouts, the *Saint-Do*, at the age of 11 in 1949, was a key moment in Pierre's human and spiritual development. He loved scouting and this activity gave him companionship and an opportunity to develop his natural aptitude for leadership. He quickly rose up through the various scouting ranks attaining all the leadership badges, including the top distinction of *écuyer de France*. His sister Anne-Marie stresses the importance of his time with the scouts, especially the summer camps where he developed 'a co-operative spirit, a sense of responsibility and a resourceful side which would stand him in good stead in later life.' [2]

The scouts were also crucial for his religious development: 'The *Saint-Do* inspired Pierre to deepen his faith, and even perhaps simply to acquire it.' [3] Pierre was nicknamed 'the attentive squirrel' by the scout leaders, a name, says Anne-Marie 'which suited him well, even as a youngster; he had a lively temperament, while at the same time being very observant and a good listener.'[4] In later life Pierre maintained many of the friendships which he had made with his fellow scouts, even though he differed from some of them in his attitude towards an independent Algeria. In fact, his final, poignant homily in France was delivered, shortly before his assassination, to former scouts of the *Saint-Do*. It was in Prouilhe, the birthplace of the Dominican Order.

Fr Louis Lefèvre OP was chaplain to the scouts and had a big influence on Pierre. A charismatic personality, he knew how to enkindle faith and to accompany the young in their search for God. However, while paying him tribute on the tenth anniversary of his death, Pierre confessed that he couldn't remember as such any of Fr Lefèvre's teaching. What he did remember was his prayerful presence which in its turn made God present and real: 'I can remember nothing ... except this profound stillness which was created around him when he prayed or presided at prayer. Close to him we were able to discover that there is pride and joy in being a Christian, without hang-ups or excessive tension.'[5]

Fr Lefèvre didn't explicitly influence Pierre in his vocation to the religious life but he did inspire him. Writing to his parents he re-assured them: 'I forgot to say that in all of this [his vocation] Fr Lefèvre had no influence on me except that which I accepted, that's to say that not for one moment did he push me to become a priest, no more than he dissuaded me from doing so.'[6] Politically, Fr Lefèvre was strongly in favour of a French Algeria, a position which Pierre came to repudiate. However, despite this disagreement, Pierre continued to maintain good personal relations with him. This warm humanity was a defining aspect of Pierre's personality and Christian life, a humanity nurtured, no doubt, by his time with the scouts.

After obtaining his baccalauréat C, an option which specialised in mathematics and the sciences, Pierre thought about entering the seminary but was discouraged from doing so by his father who advised him to first obtain a degree. Pierre followed his father's advice and enrolled in a preparatory engineering course in Algiers. Success in a competitive examination at the end of this course would have qualified him for entry into one of the specialised *Grandes Écoles*, the French equivalent of Oxford and Cambridge. Having failed his first year examination, he set out for France on 31 October, 1957 to continue his study of mathematics, physics and chemistry at Grenoble University. Apart from holidays, Pierre spent the most violent years of the war of independence outside Algeria. As the bitter urban guerrilla warfare erupted in Algiers only around the time of his departure, he escaped, for the most part, the trauma experienced by both the *pieds-noirs* and Algerians.

IN THE WILDERNESS

As a young university student Pierre defended the concept of a French Algeria, feeling that the *pieds-noirs* were misunderstood by metropolitan France. He joined a right wing student group, *Le Comité universitaire d'information politique* (CUIP, University Committee for Political Information) and was a member for one term. He even took part in an expedition to seize the left-wing weekly Catholic newspaper *Témoignage chrétien* (*Christian Witness*) which denounced the use of torture by the French in Algeria. The raiding party went on to burn copies of the newspaper in front of the bishop's residence in Grenoble. However, his political action didn't last very long and he abandoned his militancy in April 1958. An important influence in the political evolution of his thinking was the Catholic chaplaincy where a Jesuit priest, Georges Haubtman, sought to help the students develop a Christian perspective on the Algerian question.

At this time Pierre felt discouraged and somewhat lost. His heart wasn't fully in his mathematics and science studies, and he was becoming less sure of his political leanings. He decided not to pursue his studies further and instead to train for the priesthood. He broke the news to his parents in a lengthy letter which they received on 20 October 1958. Among his fellow engineering students he felt like an outsider, not sharing their technical interests and being unable to envisage a life dedicated to working in an industrial environment:

> During this year I've studied the behaviour of those working like me for this exam. I was like a stranger among them ... all are working to become engineers (with more or less ease) and strive towards this goal telling themselves that they will spend all of their lives in the midst of industrial work drawings or electric machines. All are interested to varying degrees in the same machines and in technical progress – they read *Science et Avenir* (*Science and the Future*), they build radios, or just speakers etc. Their studies, while not motivated by idealism, are their *raison d'être*.[7]

Pierre, while interested in the theoretical side of his studies, felt no attraction towards its applied side or the lifestyle which it entailed.

He told his parents about a serious relationship with a girlfriend which he would have liked to continue were it not for the competing call of religious life. He then came to his core reason for joining, if possible, the Dominicans: 'If I've chosen the priesthood – or let's call it the sacerdotal ministry – it's in order to give myself completely to something which I feel is the most beautiful thing in the world, it's to wear myself out in doing something worthwhile for others and for myself. I know what I will lose by doing so but I also know what I will gain and how it will benefit others.'[8] Pierre goes on to acknowledge the pain which his celibacy will cause his parents and re-affirms his love for them. His maturity and self-knowledge can be seen in the reasons he gives for choosing the Dominicans. He feels that the diocesan clergy have to cope with a physical and moral loneliness and although 'community life has a few drawbacks, given human nature, nevertheless it has also the huge comfort of common prayer and reflection.'[9]

FORMATION: A PERSONAL RELATIONSHIP WITH CHRIST

On 7 December 1958 Pierre entered the novitiate in Lille to begin his formation in the Dominican Order. He had 12 companions in the novitiate and was fortunate in this respect as one of the main tasks of novitiate formation is to help the novice adjust to life in community. With 12 companions Pierre would have had plenty of opportunity for coming to terms with contrasting personalities and learning how to relate to them. They also had divergent approaches to Church life, as this was a time of theological ferment in France leading up to the Second Vatican Council. In addition, many of his fellow novices had differing views on the Algerian question and would have helped Pierre to think through, from a Christian stand-point, his own understanding of the war of independence.

Jean-Jacques Pérennès OP points out that the novitiate experience was very rich: in addition to the variety of personalities and opin-ions, Pierre was also introduced to the misery of the working classes in the North of France, and to a host of interesting visiting speakers such as Marie-Dominique Chenu OP, Joseph Robert OP, the worker priest, and many others who made him aware of the theological up-heaval taking place in the Church. And all of these encounters and experiences spurred him on to devour the latest writing in theology, Scripture and spirituality.

The most important discovery of his novitiate year was that of silent prayer. The novices had half an hour of silent prayer in the morning and in the evening. In the words of Jean-Jacques Pérennès, Pierre had discovered straight away the heart of the religious life: 'While for many brothers the choral office – praying the psalms, re-cited or chanted in common several times a day – is the entry point to a regular prayer life, Pierre immediately rooted his life in a per-sonal relationship with Christ.'[10] He wrote to his parents on 24 May

1959: 'This morning at prayer I finally discovered the Trinitarian God who up until now appeared to me to be some kind of theological hairsplitting. I believe it to be the heart of Christianity: beyond the life of Jesus, of his teaching, of his Church, he [the Triune God] reveals God to us, not just as God a Father, and gives us the pattern of what we are called to be: participants in a flow of love which unites the Father to the Son, through the Spirit.'[11]

Pierre had discovered the wonders of silent prayer. Excited by this discovery, he wrote to his parents that he was confident that this time of silent prayer would become in time 'the happiness of my life.'[12] He wrote again in January 1960 about his love of prayer and its importance as a unifying force in his life: 'I am a fanatic about contemplation and I do it for an hour a day, not as one might do Greek, but in order to allow myself to live with an ongoing momentum, more and more in harmony with my chosen objective.'[13]

Pierre's commitment to prayer continued throughout his life. As a bishop he had a strict daily routine of praying the Office, silent prayer and Mass. When he preached or wrote about prayer, and the other mysteries of the Christian faith, his language was free of jargon and displayed the liveliness and conviction of someone who has a first-hand experience of God. Pierre's unflappability in the wake of the theological storms of Vatican II was built on this bedrock of daily, silent prayer. He was aware that his faith, first and foremost, depended on an encounter, the presence of Someone in his life. This encounter gave him the experience of knowing that he was unconditionally loved by God. And without this experience the Christian life can easily become a burden, rather than a joy to be savoured and shared.

BRINGING JOY TO HUMANKIND

After his simple profession on 8 December 1959, Pierre left the novitiate and entered the Dominican house of studies, *Le Saulchoir*, where he would pursue his philosophical and theological studies until 1967 (apart from 18 months of military service, which began in March 1962). A thriving Dominican community of 153 religious awaited him, 70 of whom were in formation. This house of studies had seen the great theological masters and precursors of Vatican II, Yves Congar OP and Marie-Dominique Chenu OP, teach within its walls.[14] The *studium* breathed the theological excitement and thinking which came to fruition in the Council documents. In other words, Pierre was a participant in an important moment of renewal in the Church's theological self-understanding.

Moreover, his superiors, recognizing his personal maturity, appointed him to leadership roles within the student body, initially as dean of the student brothers and then of the young priests. In his letters to his parents, which were amazingly frank and open, he shared his bourgeoning faith, a faith which they were beginning to discover too in all its richness. In his Easter letter on 2 April 1961, Pierre, barely 23 years of age, wrote: 'To be sure of the power of the Father's Love, that's the message of Easter ... It is this certainty lived out to its logical conclusion which makes martyrs and which means that we, Christians, must bring joy to mankind, whatever may be the cross which we have to bear. All of the Christian message is in these lines: abandonment to the will of the Father who is love.'[15]

Pierre at Le Saulchoir, *16 December 1959*

On 14 February 1965 Pierre, in a letter to his family, outlined his understanding of his life as a Dominican friar. He had been asked, as part of his homiletic training, to sum up the purpose of religious life. What he wrote on this occasion, he noted, was more or less identical to his reflections before solemn profession on 1 November 1964, almost a year earlier:

1. The background to my vocation is the shock of the Algerian war with the ensuing turmoil it provoked in the Christian conscience. 2. I therefore entered religious life to find clarity in my life, strengthened by a fundamental intuition: to find Christ = to find the meaning of life. 3. Hence the primary desire to be 'a man of God' in the way that Islam still understands it – who lives from God and for God, understood fairly concretely as a life companion, a person such as he was on earth, and continues to be, I believe. I make this presence the framework of my life, consciously sought in a familiarity with what he has revealed explicitly of himself (in the Bible and the life of the Church), with what he reveals in 'the secret of the heart' to a life which is as open as possible to his word, ever new. In concrete terms, I feel alive when I'm stretching towards God and towards others. 4. From this comes also the need to explain and to communicate what I feel in living this out. I only really come alive when demands are made upon me: this includes a conscious determination to be open to people and to history in the making, of attentiveness. 5. As regards my life as a religious: my desire to be a 'man of God', according to my specific way of life (others will fulfil this desire in marriage, for example), takes shape in a life of prayer, stretching as much as possible towards the heart of things and towards people (liturgical life, community life, openness to the world), and given as completely as possible to what is the main focus of my life, (the vows). My need to communicate is fulfilled in a life

consecrated to deciphering the meaning of events in the light of faith and of the Revelation of Jesus Christ (a life of study).[16]

This summary is a very concise and accurate outline of his future life and ministry. Pierre knew himself well – his need for an intimate life of prayer, for a strong relationship with God and with other people. He was what one might call a 'man of relationship'; he could only function well when he was in relationship and giving fully of himself to God and to others. Pierre's image of his life as a Dominican, one of stretching out to God and to others, is a premonition of what his fidelity to the suffering Christ will entail – being stretched out on the cross, on the 'fault lines' of a suffering humanity, in order that others might know God's love for them. As we shall see later, Pierre went on to lead a very active life in priestly ministry, some might even call it frenetic. The incessant demands and challenges which he faced suited his temperament and brought him life. He was called to be a contemplative in action, open to the world, in other words to be a good Dominican friar. Underpinning all of this activity was the fundamental intuition and experience that Christ alone could give his life meaning and this meaning was love.

THE CROSS OF CHRIST

As his letters home show, during his time as a novice and student, Pierre had an exceptionally mature understanding of his faith. His compass was the life, death and resurrection of Jesus which he sought to live out in his own life. Following a crucified Jesus, says Pierre, not only involves the big choices in life such as becoming a religious, but also the little free choices of everyday life. It is in this way that we help to bring in the Kingdom in the here and now: 'Between the ways of men and the ways of God there is this unfathomable mystery of the Cross and if one accepts to be shaped by it, one can hope for a resurrection. The Cross isn't any old suffering, it's not even suffering *per se*. It's this continuous desire to always choose in harmony with God; it's to break 'our hearts of stone and our stiff necks', as the Bible says. ... And all of this can be summed up in four words, to follow Jesus Christ, to try to look at life and at others through his eyes; and this is a great strength, much stronger than a moral law (which it implies but which it so surpasses!).' [17]

The centrality and inescapability of the cross was key to Pierre's spirituality throughout his life and would form the central point of his last public homily at Prouilhe. In one of the final retreats he gave, in 1992, on St Paul, *Avec Saint Paul*[18] he talks about Jesus' refusal to engage in violence and the desire for power. St Paul, writes Pierre, discovers in the cross of Christ a place of pardon and forgiveness, the reconciliation of humankind with God. Jesus, the innocent victim 'reveals then all the sin which lives in the human heart (ours – cowardice, betrayal, contempt, rejection of the other, derision, desire for power, political intrigue, personal interests to be protected) and which undoes creation.' [19]

By his death on the cross Jesus reveals to us a God of love. However, it wasn't only on the cross that Jesus revealed to us a God of love. He also did so in his teaching, healing and forgiving; Jesus revealed to us that God's life is a life of self-giving love. And love respects the freedom of others and in so doing becomes weak, vulnerable and humble: 'What is revealed on the Cross? Someone who, rejected by the forces of evil, the forces of death, will surrender himself in forgiveness, will enter into suffering and death, without holding anything back, giving himself away.' [20] Out of love Jesus refuses all violence, all coercion. His only weapons in the struggle with evil are the weapons of defenceless love. By taking upon himself hatred, rejection and exclusion, the sin of the world, Jesus breaks the vicious circle of violence and shows forth God's glory. And it was precisely this gratuitous love, shown on the Cross by Jesus, which (as Pierre would later come to see), was the main reason for the Church's refusal to abandon a war torn Algeria.

THE EXCLUSION OF THE OTHER

During his time at *Le Saulchoir* Pierre became more conscious of his *pied-noir* background and of his difference from the mainland French. On 29 February 1960 he wrote to his parents: 'You can't begin to imagine how much I would like to go back to Algiers. I'm beginning to realise that I'm literally of "another race" from the people here – whatever the proponents of an "Algeria-French" province may think. Perhaps we are a French province but if so a very meridional and Mediterranean one – in any case one which has nothing to do with our Nordic brothers. That doesn't mean that I don't love them. No. But I realise that I must disconcert them quite a lot by my reactions just as they exasperate me sometimes by their unwavering seriousness. In fact, what is missing here is the sun. Perhaps with the summer they will defrost. When all is said and done, I couldn't care less. I've got some sunshine within me and that is enough.' [21]

With time, and especially after joining the Dominicans, the full reality of what the *pied-noir* outlook implied dawned on him: it was a political and cultural stance based on the exclusion of the other who was different: different in religion, different in language and different in culture. This evolution in Pierre's thinking appears to have been quite rapid. Just one month after his arrival in the novitiate, in his Christmas 1958 letter to his parents, he talks about ministering in Algiers, learning Arabic and studying Islam.[22] In the Dominican environment of prayer and study, preaching and fellowship, Pierre had found the compass which would direct his course for the rest of his life and lead him to a deeper knowledge and love of his homeland. The sacrifice which he had made in entering the Dominicans would bear a rich harvest.

Writing to his brothers in the Dominican Order in 1981 to announce his appointment as Bishop of Oran, Pierre spoke of his twofold vocation to Algeria and to the Dominicans. Little by little he became convinced of two things. Firstly, the colonial set-up rendered relationships with their Algerian neighbours well-nigh impossible, weighing upon the *pieds-noirs* like a kind of original sin: 'The colonial mortgage weighed upon our world like a kind of original sin, blighting all our behaviour and our best good will, blighting our Christian undertakings. We were collectively condemned to live among ourselves and to dominate in order to survive. The second conviction was born from the shock of the first: it was necessary to break down walls, to put human beings, peoples, and their cultures in communication with each other.' [23]

Pierre's 'thirst to communicate', born out of his segregated colonial existence, found its natural outlet in the Dominican way of life. By joining the Order he was enabled to understand and come to terms with his colonial past. He was haunted by the realisation that he, and most of the colonial Church in Algeria, had completely misunderstood the Gospel imperative of reaching out to one's neighbour, especially to the marginalised and powerless. He writes to his brothers: 'I was then thirsty to understand how we had been able to live, and live in a Christian manner, without even asking ourselves about the other, the stranger, while the whole of the Gospel resonated with his cry, condemning all Pharisaical separation. The urgency of a word became clear to me, hesitantly, in the theological tumult where I was carving out a difficult path. An evangelical word born out of an evangelical life. An evangelical life founded on a word truly received from God, discerned, prayed.' [24]

His dawning realisation in his first year as a mathematics and science student at the University of Grenoble that the *pieds-noirs,* and more especially he himself, had gone astray in their understanding of their presence in Algeria was *the* turning point of his spiritual life. Pierre's gradual awakening to the reality of the Algerian other was the experience which underpinned all of his priestly ministry:

This was the beginning of my religious vocation. It was necessary to make the Word of God heard in the events of history

and above all – and above all! – break down the walls, open
the frontiers, never again to close one's eyes, one's ears. On
the contrary, to know the other, to move towards the other,
and in order to do that to move out of one's bubble. A bitter
and salutary experience. God became for me the God of the
Exodus. From then on I was aware of the nature of 'collective
sin' or what John-Paul II called 'structural sin' in his social
encyclical. To be caught up in an environment or in such a
social, economic or political structure, for which one is not
personally responsible, involves participating in an unjust
situation. From the day that a French soldier set foot in Algeria, everything was set in motion, culminating in the years of
violence. [25]

4

Life as a Dominican Friar

ARE Dominicans apostolic or contemplative? Traditionally the
Dominicans have used the Latin tag *contemplata aliis tradere* –
to take to others the fruits of our contemplation – to describe their
way of life. However, the male branch of the Order has always had a
strong pull towards action at the expense of contemplation. This has
been compounded by a tendency, says Pierre, to make the excuse
that prayer and life are linked and that therefore their active life is
also prayer. Pierre is not convinced by this reasoning. Life is neutral.
It can lead both to death and life. If their life is only ceaseless activity
and agitation then they are merely surviving, they are not giving life
to others: 'And, precisely, if we wish our life to be truly fruitful, it will
be very necessary for the Spirit to transform what is sterile in us into
fruitfulness! And that is contemplation: it is to allow the Spirit to
transform in us our inner sterilities, deaths, refusals, and rigidities
into fruitfulness, to give the Spirit scope.'[1]

Silent prayer was indispensable in Pierre's own life, as also was
community prayer. What unifies the community, says Pierre, is not
the organisation of its work, generosity, personal affinity, or the
physical building but rather the One who calls the members together. They discover their unity in being attentive together to God's call
and in celebrating Him: 'Prayer is a disposition to receive together,
a disposition to listen, a disposition to welcome. Meetings cannot

replace the call of God to decipher together, to listen together, to celebrate together.'[2] In community life praying together is a non-negotiable because it helps to discern God's presence which alone can unite the community.

Priestly life as a Dominican friar got off to a good start for Pierre. He was very happy with the lifestyle of the Dominican community in Algiers.[3] He found working as part of a small community more natural and satisfying than being part of a larger community in one of the bigger French friaries. Living in an apartment in the midst of everyday life was also more to his liking than the more isolated, monastic style of life at *Le Saulchoir*. The brethren still maintained a rhythm of prayer, saying the Office when they were together: 'Common prayer, work and service in fraternal teams, I couldn't ask anything more from the Order.'[4]

His hectic and irregular schedule meant that he and his fellow friars had difficulty in meeting for meals, Mass or the Office. Pierre outlined, in February 1970, the obstacles which they encountered in sharing community worship and life. They, *i.e.*, Pierre Le Baut, François Chavanes and Jean-Pierre Voreux, all worked outside the community and they all had different timetables. The week-end was almost their only opportunity for being together. Such an active lifestyle, with inevitable repercussions on the quality of community life, was not ideal. The superior, Pierre Le Baut, left the community in November 1972, at the age of 48, to get married to an Algerian widow. In a letter to Pierre in October 1974, his sister, Anne-Marie, commented perceptively on his need for relaxation which the family holiday had just provided: 'One can take the time to look at one's life, to get things in perspective and I'm sure that you need this; how on earth do you reconcile your duties and your "interior" life?'[5] While director of the diocesan pastoral and study centre, *Les Glycines* (1973-81), where he resided, his contact with his community was even more reduced. He writes in June 1973: 'Finally a day of rest at No 92 with the brethren. I haven't seen them together for almost three weeks!'[6]

A FRENZIED SCHEDULE

One thing which stands out in all his letters (apart from frequent references to the weather) is his busy and exhausting schedule: studying and teaching Arabic, translating articles from Arabic for the *Revue de Presse,* translating ibn Rushd (Averroès), giving retreats and conferences, preaching on the Sunday radio Mass, being a dean in the archdiocese, delivering theological and pastoral talks to parishes and various religious congregations and ecumenical groups,[7] providing pastoral support to various individuals, frequently dining out with friends and work colleagues, including one evening a week with the Lebanese sisters. One wonders how he managed to maintain a life of community and prayer in the midst of such a rhythm of relentless activity. Mgr Teissier commented in an e-mail to me: 'Pierre was part of a very large number of pastoral, intellectual, political and spiritual projects. He was a very fluent speaker and could have given a new talk to his community almost every day. He met everyone where they were and never refused to help out with a lecture or a written reflection.'[8]

His ever-wise father wrote to him in November 1968 that he was concerned by his overloaded timetable and reminded him of the need for silence, balance and moderation in his lifestyle: 'It is obviously your job ... not to live for yourself, but more than for the rest of us it is indispensable to enter into the silence of your heart in order to focus your energies and your abilities. ... Everything should tend towards a wise moderation and balance. And this is all the more true for you taking into account your impulsive, or even nervous, temperament.'[9]

On New Year's Day, 1974 Pierre reflects on his hectic lifestyle where he is being pulled in many directions with the consequent risk of living on the surface of life. The two aspects of his Dominican vocation are in constant tension, namely, the contemplative and the active: 'My dream, believe it or not, is to be a Trappist somewhere and to centre my life on what I suspect is its most important element and, finally, the most necessary for others. And then I find myself "thrown on the road". This must be a sign of a Dominican vocation, this contradiction continually being lived out between two aspects of the same vocation.' [10]

This frenetic pace of life reached its climax when he reluctantly agreed to become Mgr Scotto's theological adviser in the diocese of Constantine and Hippone, in the north east of the country, in November 1970. It was agreed that each month he would spend three weeks in Constantine and one in Algiers. This would enable him to continue teaching Arabic grammar in the courses run by the Lebanese sisters. Pierre was also adamant that his own Arabic studies for the *licence* (BA) in Aix-en-Provence should be maintained. His study of Arabic, language and culture was of paramount importance for him and it was his firm desire that it should remain 'the key focus of my religious and intellectual life.' [11] In October 1972 he announced to his parents that he had passed his primary degree in Arabic at Aix-en-Provence with '*mention bien*' (good) and that he now intended to work for his master's. However, there is no further reference in his letters to his having continued with his studies at Aix-en-Provence. This is not surprising given the extent of his commitments and heavy workload. After one year he decided that he could no longer sustain the burden of work involved in commuting between Constantine and Algiers each month. He handed in his resignation to Mgr Scotto who had no option but graciously to accept Pierre's departure in September 1971.

RESPONDING TO MANY DEMANDS

Pierre was elected to the Priests' Council in November 1972, and subsequently he was one of three elected to the steering committee. After a year in post he resigned but was re-elected, against his will, the following year. He was also a member of the Order's provincial council which required regular trips to Paris. In December 1972 Pierre's responsibilities were further increased when he was unanimously elected director of the Diocesan Pastoral and Study Centre, *Les Glycines*, to succeed Fr Henri Teissier who had been appointed Bishop of Oran.

Pierre describes the work of the centre as follows: 'This pastoral and language centre is a large house which accommodates six permanent staff (theologians, linguists and bursary) and the students of dialectal Arabic. It's from here that the Arabic courses, the theology sessions and the diocesan pastoral programme are organised.'[12] The work of the Centre also included interreligious dialogue and courses on Arabic culture and civilisation. Directing and animating this impressive range of courses and events would take up most of his time and energy until he was nominated in October 1981 to succeed Mgr Teissier as Bishop of Oran.

In November 1978 Pierre reluctantly agreed, given his overcrowded timetable, to act as President of the Protestant social development agency, *Rencontres et Développement* (*Encounter and Development*), having been unanimously elected to this post.

In the retreat entitled, 'I Didn't Know My Name' (*Je ne savais pas mon nom*) given to religious and written sometime in 1979/80 Pierre adopts the persona of an anonymous religious sister, putting into her mouth the various joys and challenges of living in community. And he has her tell of a time in her life when she no longer prayed because her life was too full of activity, of human satisfactions of all kinds. I suspect that some of what he said, about her hectic lifestyle and its negative effects, could refer to his own experience: 'I no longer even thought of saying thank you and I had nothing to ask for I was so fulfilled. Totally given over to appearances, I almost died interiorly from that huge void which I thought was full because I thought I was living it for God. I have just got over it now that I have returned to a more modest life – simpler and humbler ... more human also perhaps. Yes, prayer is a vital necessity once we realise that everything is to be received, that we do nothing good if we don't receive ourselves from God and that everything is gift.' [13]

When I asked several people who knew him well at this time if Pierre gave the impression of leading a slightly unbalanced lifestyle, they all replied in the negative. His first priority was prayer, especially personal prayer. Bishop Claude Rault wrote to me: 'He had a quite intense and deep personal prayer life. This could be seen in his life and in his writings. He had a great passion for the Gospel and like a true Dominican, he knew how to put over the message.' And Mgr Henri Teissier, a close friend, wrote: 'His life of prayer took pride of place. Up early, he went down to his chapel and took time for personal prayer, recitation of the Office and the celebration of Mass.' They all commented on how well organised he was, and ,according to his Vicar General in Oran, Thierry Becker: 'He gave no impression whatsoever of being frenetic; on the contrary, [he gave the impression] of being amazingly balanced.'

PREACHER AND RETREAT-GIVER

Pierre Claverie was, above all, a Dominican friar. The followers of St Dominic have a clear identity. They are called to lead lives of prayer and study in community and to share the fruits of their lives with others through preaching and scholarship. He was always willing to accept an invitation to preach and saw this as a challenge to read up on subjects with which he was unfamiliar. On his death 95 folders were discovered with preaching texts and preparatory notes taken from various books and articles. The first 84 of the dossiers had titles given by Pierre. The homilies were often handwritten and showed no crossing out.

Pierre was recognised by his superiors as a gifted preacher and

on his arrival in Algiers in 1967 he was appointed by his prior, Pierre
Le Baut, to preach the Sunday homilies on Radio Alger. He shared
this task at first with a few other Dominicans, the team of preachers
being later enlarged to include diocesan clergy. Pierre received positive feedback, especially from his parents who were glued to their
radio in Nice, the reception varying from week to week. After his
first radio homily he wondered if it hadn't been 'too dense' and the
tone 'a little pompous.'[14]

Pierre spent a month each summer giving retreats, mainly to religious sisters and on occasion to bishops, lay people and to *Caritas
Christi*, an international secular institute. The majority of these retreats were given in Algeria, the Lebanon and later in Martinique,
but he also gave retreats in Nigeria and Canada. He tells us that in
Algeria he couldn't preach in the streets: 'Well, it's for that reason
that, from time to time, leaving the Muslim world, I speak, I enjoy
myself. That's to say, sincerely, that I rediscover the savour of being
a Christian in that experience.'[15]

Unusually, he regarded this activity as part of his holidays. Fr
Thierry Becker was worried about Pierre not taking any holidays
apart from short stays with his parents. When he mentioned this
to him, Pierre replied that 'his rest was found in the retreats which
he preached.'[16] Writing to his parents from Constantine in August
1969, while giving a retreat to 30 sisters from various congregations,
he describes his challenging daily timetable: 7.30 –8.00 Self-service
breakfast; 8.15 Lauds; 8.30–9.30 Conference; 10.00–11.00 Round
table; 11.30 Mass with homily; 12.15 Lunch; 14.00–16.00 Meeting
individual sisters; 16.00–7.00 Second round table; 17.30–18.30 Conference; 19.00 Vespers; 19.15 Dinner. After dinner he went home to
prepare for the following day.

Another unusual feature of his life when he was Bishop of Oran
was his custom of giving his diocesan priests their yearly retreat.
Most bishops, I imagine, would give their priests a retreat once
or twice during their time in office. This showed, on Pierre's part,

a great love of preaching and a desire to grow closer to his clergy. With just about 35 priests in his diocese he would have known each one of them intimately. Whether it was a good idea to give his clergy a retreat every year could be questioned.

MARKED BY THIS VOCATION OF A PREACHER

The archives in Oran contain texts for 16 different week-long retreats preached between 1968 and 1995.[17] The same retreat was usually preached three or four times, being modified a little on each occasion or conflated with another retreat. However, his retreat on interreligious dialogue was given on about 12 occasions. He preached on a wide number of topics including religious life, Our Lady, spirituality/theology, Islam, interreligious dialogue, social justice; and one of his final retreats was given on St Paul. In one of his letters he remarks, that when giving a retreat he tended to be anxious and on edge during the first few days but would end up being surprised by how well his preaching had been received.

Although his conferences didn't rely very much on personal anecdotes, he liked to tell some wisdom stories drawn from, among others, Hampate Ba, a Malian Muslim mystic whom Pierre had met in the Niger. Other authors whom he quotes, from time to time, include the Breton priest and novelist, Jean Sulivan, the French Jesuit theologian, François Varillon, and the fourteenth century German mystic and Dominican friar, Meister Eckhart. While a student Pierre enjoyed studying St Thomas Aquinas, the most influential Dominican theologian of all time. Surprisingly, he appears to rarely quote St Thomas except with reference to his statement that the perfection of charity is the only purpose of religious life.[18]

Although Pierre in his retreat preaching seldom related stories from his own life it was obvious that his preaching was based on his lived experience of the Christian life. For example, in preaching about the vows he has this to say: 'If we truly live the spirit of poverty and of chastity we will be open, attentive, welcoming and respectful of everyone, ready for encounter, because we are without barriers and defences.'[19] It would be difficult to find a better description of Pierre himself. Pierre Claverie's preaching carried the ring of truth because it was the fruit of his own prayer and striving to live out the Gospel in daily life.

Pierre found that his constant preaching and lecturing, and the reflection which this demanded, helped to keep his faith alive: 'It's strange to note how much I'm marked by this vocation of a "preacher"! Others could live in silence: I almost physically experience the necessity to express the content of my faith, for myself, first of all, and to enter into relation with the other Christians who are travelling with me in the footsteps of Christ in Algeria. All of that is fairly fascinating and really is worth living.'[20] I, for one, am glad that Pierre chose to become a preacher rather than a silent Trappist.

5

··

The Challenges of an Evangelical Life

ST DOMINIC, the founder of the Order of Preachers, held steadfastly, comments Pierre, to the practice and spirit of poverty
because he understood that poverty of spirit and means were necessary in order to give to others what's most important, the gift of
self. St Dominic forced a bursar to stop work on improving the cells
of the brothers with the words: 'Do you already wish to renounce
poverty and construct big palaces?'[1] Pierre never forgot this excla-
mation. All our works, he wrote, however important or substantial,
must remain close to people and allow for a sense of sharing and
solidarity. And for this to happen 'it is important to rely first of all
upon one's inner strength and not on external means. Even if we are
called upon to direct important works let these works be built first
of all upon the inner strength of our communities and members.'[2]
For Pierre, it was the inner, spiritual dynamism behind the projects
that mattered. This spiritual strength allows Christian communities
not only to persevere but also to transmit something lasting, regardless of the means being employed. In other words, for Pierre, the
apostolate must have as its bedrock life in the Spirit.

The vow of poverty is a reminder that we can live simply without
surrounding ourselves with gadgets and a multiplicity of possessions and consumer goods, without becoming enslaved to money.
It is also a sign of solidarity with the poor and a reminder that the
goods of this world belong to everyone, that sharing comes before

private property. According to Pierre, the vow of poverty is a great act of faith, freeing us from the idolatry of money and freeing us also for more human, loving relationships where people take precedence over possessions. We require inner strength to simply be ourselves without the protection which wealth provides. Our attitude towards money, observes Pierre, tells us very clearly about our commitment to God: 'Our behaviour towards money tells us who we are, it is the test of our truthfulness, whatever may be the amount which we have to manage. We can be rich with 20 pence if we treasure it as the most important thing in our lives. Our behaviour, our way of handling money tells us our way of being with God; this test is infallible.'[3]

This clear and strong statement is revealing of Pierre's own spiritual practice. Pierre lived a very simple existence and people were amazed to find, following his assassination, that all his belongings fitted into two small suitcases. Our attitude towards money and possession appears to be, for him, the key indicator of our relationship with God. Does God come first? Or do idols usurp his place in our lives? The accumulation of objects and possessions is a primary temptation, the one which the traditional religious vow of poverty sought to counter. The reason why we seek to surround ourselves with possessions of various kinds, says Pierre, is a sign of a crisis of faith, of a lack of confidence in God and in ourselves, of an inner loneliness. On account of this inner fragility we look for security in our possessions: 'We surround ourselves with objects because we have no inner existence or because we have the impression of being too fragile. One has to be really strong to simply accept oneself, without masks, without defence, in simplicity, in poverty.'[4]

OPEN HANDS AND OPEN HEART

The most important witness which we can give, Pierre remarks, is the 'density' of our being which radiates God's glory dwelling within us. Pierre liked to quote in his retreats the great Dominican theologian and mystic, Meister Eckhart, and his influence can be seen in Pierre's teaching about the evangelical counsels. Meister Eckhart writes: 'People ought to think less about what they do and more about who they are. If people were good in their being, the works which they do would shine in abundance. If you are just, your acts are also just. Sanctity doesn't lie in doing, it emanates from being, for it is not works which sanctify us but we who sanctify works.'[5] Like Eckhart, Pierre points out that it is only when our works and projects flow out of the goodness of our inner selves that they will bear lasting fruit. What is important is to be rooted in God, possessing his Spirit, the source of all our goodness. It is only then that our lives will become truly fruitful: 'The prophets repeat throughout salvation history: Beware of words, beware of rites, beware of laws, beware of all that is merely empty words or simply human regulations. What's important is the density of your being and the quality of your life.'[6]

The gifts which we have been given through the Holy Spirit and through the Spirit in the lives of others must in their turn be shared: 'The life which I receive multiplies itself in being shared.'[7] Pierre drew concrete consequences from this for his own life. First of all, he wished to live with open hands and an open heart, so that he could welcome others into his life. Accordingly, he always kept the door of his office open to avoid becoming absorbed in his own plans and projects to the exclusion of others. Secondly, he wished by this practice to become humble, to receive God himself in welcoming others: 'I must absolutely empty myself of all that clutters my inner space ... and exterior also. Humility consists not in despising oneself, of putting oneself in a mouse hole, as Bernanos puts it, but in arranging a space where I don't hold centre stage, where I don't prevent others from entering.'[8]

In this way, says Pierre, by giving others our full attention, by recognising their existence we let them know that they are valued, that they exist in our eyes: 'Humility is about entering into a fraternal relationship with others and not a dominating, seductive or invasive one. And the key to humility is voluntary poverty, it is to accept to be poor in one's claims on the other. Concretely this means paying attention to the other person, whereas too often we live in indifference side by side because we know each other too well.'[9] Each one of us, in encountering God's presence in our own lives, is called to share that presence with others, a presence which gives confidence to the other and releases new life in them. By being flexible and available, Pierre sought to leave room for the unexpected, for God to intervene in the concrete and unforeseen events of his everyday life, to disrupt his routines so that his heart might be enlarged and become more welcoming to others.

REMAINING DISSATISFIED

The danger for communities and people who have everything is similar to that which the rich man encountered when faced by Lazarus, the poor beggar at his gate.[10] The rich man, says Pierre, just couldn't see Lazarus' plight because he himself had all his needs satisfied. People who have all their needs met, and have everything they want, can't even begin to imagine what it means to be materially poor: 'It is not bad will, one doesn't see any more. I am convinced that a certain way of living blinds, imprisons, possesses to such an extent that one no longer hears entreaties, that one no longer sees those who are different.'[11]

Christians and religious communities must avoid becoming like the rich man in his blindness. Pierre believes that religious communities can easily become complacent and self-satisfied. So they must seek to challenge this complacency and self-sufficiency. In our search for God we will never arrive; we must always be on the way. We require 'a thorn in the flesh'[12] to keep our search alive, 'a minimum of desire, some thirst, which obliges us not to remain in our complacency.'[13] Otherwise, we will die spiritually. Without some desire on our part there is no room for God to act in our lives. So we must try to deepen this desire for God through fasting and simple living.

Our culture is fixated on material possessions, on objects, and is strongly individualistic. If we buy into these values, comments Pierre, then we have nothing to offer to young people who are searching for something different. Young people, sated on material things, are left rudderless, without spiritual resources: 'Well, we [religious communities] are in league with this situation, we have built on sand by developing individualism, egoism and the search for tranquillity. I believe we really need to find anew the meaning of effort, of privation, of self-transcendence to overcome this crisis which isn't only an economic one: it is a crisis of humanity.' [14]

For a consecrated religious, the fruitfulness of their lives will depend to a large extent on their ability to live the 'thorn in the flesh', the incompleteness which celibacy entails. Chastity cannot be lived separately from other two traditional vows of poverty, and obedience,[15] says Pierre, as they are all concerned with self-denial, self-surrender so that a person can offer something of themselves to others. Pierre remarked that whenever he experienced difficulty with some aspect of the vow of chastity he saw this as an indication that there was something amiss in his living out of the other two evangelical counsels as the three vows are interlinked and stand or fall together.[16] Chastity touches the deepest part of our being, there where we meet our desire: 'If faith hasn't reached us at the heart of our desire, if it doesn't convert also our desire a little, then we will remain prisoners for the rest of our life.' [17] The vow of chastity, he commented, 'will only carry meaning if it shows itself in a free, open, receptive, attentive, and welcoming attitude' [18] towards others. In living celibacy fruitfully religious give a clear witness to the power of the Spirit at work in their lives.

OBEDIENCE?

Living in community demands the ability to adjust to many different kinds of temperaments and personalities and also the ability
to listen and put the common good before one's own preferences.
For Pierre, this was sometimes a challenge. In May 1968 one of his
sermons on Radio Alger was judged to be controversial and he was
called in by Mgr Jacquier, the auxiliary bishop of Algiers, to explain
himself. Pierre, in a letter to his parents, defended himself vigorous-
ly on the grounds that his homily was in perfect agreement with the
teaching of the Second Vatican Council: 'I am absolutely certain of
being in the right and I won't give way an inch on the substance.'[19]
Elsewhere, he refers a little dismissively to Fr Teissier's[20] sense of
obedience: 'I like Teissier – who is remarkably intelligent – a lot: but
like many diocesans he is formed in a mystique of obedience to the
bishop which influences considerably his judgement.'[21]

I think it would be true to say that Pierre had a very independent mind-set and, once he had made up his mind, he was not
easily knocked off course by ecclesiastical authority. This could be
explained by the devolved sense of authority which is part of the
Dominican charism and lifestyle and also partly by Pierre's personality. In a letter to the Dominican Order, the then Master, Fr Timothy Radcliffe, wrote that Dominicans right from the beginning had
a democratic approach to decision making: 'From the beginning
of the Order we have arrived at these decisions democratically, by
debate leading to voting. But what makes this democratic process
properly Dominican is that we are not merely seeking to discover
what is the will of the majority, but what are the needs of the mission. To what mission are we sent?'[22] The more hierarchical and less
consultative approach of diocesan government, where decisions
came more from the top down, didn't appeal to Pierre.

This can be seen in his refusal to remain on the Priests' Council
for the Archdiocese of Algiers after one year's service. He doesn't

state his reasons for resigning in his letters home but I think it's likely, drawing on the general tone of his comments in other letters, that he felt he wasn't achieving a great deal and that the real decisions were being taken at a higher level. In December 1969 Pierre commented in a letter to his parents: 'Nothing out of the ordinary, except that the bishop [Duval] is determined to hold on to all the power and all authority; in these conditions one wonders why there are so many "advisory bodies" and "commissions".' [23] Despite the Cardinal's refusal to accept his resignation, he withdrew from the meetings of this body. In addition, he had no hesitation in leaving Constantine after one year once he had decided that this was the right course of action, despite the setback which this decision must have caused Mgr Scotto.

HELPING PEOPLE TO GROW

In September 1978, the Provincial of France and the Master of Dominican Order made strenuous efforts to appoint Pierre prior of their house in Cairo. This renowned house of studies lacked leadership and a clear sense of direction. Pierre was considered to be the ideal person to put it on a sound footing, given his knowledge of Arabic and his natural gifts for leadership. The Provincial also intended to send Régis Morelon to Cairo with Pierre. Pierre comments that the Algiers brethren 'are obviously shattered because it means the end of our presence in Algiers if you remove the two Arab speakers from the house.' [24]

Pierre fought a determined battle, enlisting the support of the Cardinal and others, to thwart these efforts and through his diplomatic skills managed to stay put in Algiers. He comments: 'I wrote to the Provincial that I was nevertheless ready to go there [to Cairo], should it be absolutely necessary and under obedience; this would involve my receiving a formal order (we call this in the jargon, a formal precept) to leave Algeria. I am asking for that because, reason-

ably, from my point of view, I find this decision irrational.'[25] On his
return to Algeria in 1967, now ordained as a priest, Pierre had spent
his time building friendships with his Muslim compatriots. These
relationships required time and perseverance in order to overcome
the suspicions and reticence brought about by a colonial past. And
now the fruit of all this labour of love was being endangered. He
wrote to one of the collaborators of the Master of the Order in Rome:
'I've spent ten years in a country where personal relationships are
our only strength because we haven't got any institutions; and God
only knows that these relationships take a long time to establish and
remain fragile. They demand time, patience and mean a lot to our
Algerian friends.'[26] His commitment to Algeria and the Algerian
Church were not to be taken lightly.

In one of his retreat conferences Pierre talked about the difficulties he experienced with obedience in his own life.[27] He comments
that the Latin root of the word 'authority', *auctoritas,* comes from
augere which means to grow. So exercising authority, in the etymo-
logical sense, entails helping someone to grow and in the case of
a religious, helping them to grow in their vocation. Very often, he
comments, religious are resistant to change and find it difficult to
respond to their superiors' decision to give them a new job or to
move them to a new community. Pierre experienced this situation
on two occasions. In addition to being asked to go to Cairo, a year
later he was asked to move to France. On both occasions he outlined
his reasons for wishing to stay in Algeria as he thought it was the
place where his talents and experience could be best utilised. And
on both occasions his superiors had accepted his reasoning. However, he recognised that he needed to ask himself if the reasons he
had given were genuine or whether they had concealed a wish, on
his part, not to be disturbed. In any case, he made it clear to his superiors that he would leave Algeria immediately should they reject
his reasoning. He wryly concludes that it is difficult being a superior
as 'we [the other members of the community] do not really wish to

grow.' [28]

In his relationship with Cardinal Duval one can see Pierre's frustration with what he considered to be an outdated exercise of authority, allied to an overly hierarchical notion of the Church. At the beginning of his priestly ministry Pierre's relationship with the Cardinal wasn't particularly warm. He found him to be old-fashioned in his approach to authority, somewhat of a prince of the Church who expected unquestioning obedience. He recounts a meeting with Cardinal Duval and the Diocesan Council of Priests. When Pierre challenged the Cardinal about his proposed enforcement of some liturgical norms (which everyone ignored), Pierre was frustrated by the Cardinal's refusal to discuss the matter. Cardinal Duval replied that he was simply obeying the Pope. Pierre wonders: 'How can such a great man be so stuck when it is a question of the church apparatus: that's exactly what I fear when people speak about the episcopacy: to become conditioned to such an extent that one is no longer able, that one no longer wishes to see reality.' [29]

However, as time went by he became more positive in his attitude to the Cardinal and began to appreciate more his wisdom and perseverance in the face of many political difficulties.

AN INDEPENDENT SPIRIT

Pierre was a born leader and the role of follower did not suit him. He had a clear vision of what the mission of the Church in Algeria was about and he liked to see practical measures and changes being implemented rather than endless discussions and meetings which led nowhere. On account of Pierre's unusual inner strength and self-confidence he related easily to others.

The downside of this virtue was, at times, a self-assurance which didn't easily give way to an opposing viewpoint. This can be seen in his refusal, unless he were to be formally ordered to do so, to move either to Cairo or to France as requested by his superiors. This independent spirit was also noted by the military chaplain in charge of Pierre during his military service. In an otherwise laudatory report which commented on his generosity and solid piety, the chaplain noted 'an independence of spirit which makes it difficult for him to accept the point of view of others.'[30]

In his book *Pierre Claverie Un Algérien par alliance*, his confrère Jean-Jacques Pérennès OP gives us a thorough account of Pierre's life. He had worked with him in Algeria and knew him very well. Jean-Jacques, like everyone who knew Pierre, admired him greatly and respected his humanity and integrity. Pérennès goes on to comment that the most accurate judgement regarding Pierre's independent spirit was surely that of François Chavanes, a Dominican friar and priest who had known Pierre since he was a 16-year-old boy scout in Algiers: 'Pierre was someone over whom one really had no influence.'[31] In other words Pierre was someone who knew his own mind so well that it was difficult to modify his viewpoint.

At the same time Jean-Jacques notes that one of Pierre's characteristics was 'an intimate aversion to ideological confrontation, at the risk of sometimes appearing ambiguous. He believed more in human relationships than in very abstract debates.'[32] For example, Pierre avoided confrontation with his former boy scout chaplain, Fr Lefèvre, who was a partisan of a French Algeria. This was because Pierre valued relationship more than ideas. He could distinguish the person whom he loved from the ideas with which he disagreed. However, this doesn't imply that he wouldn't stand up for the ideas and principles in which he believed. By refusing to be moved to Cairo or France, he had stood firm in his vocation to work for reconciliation in Algeria, to make reparation for the indifference and arrogance with which the Algerians had been treated by the *pieds-noirs*. His vocation as a Christian was to 'to break down walls, to put human beings, peoples, and their cultures in communication with each other.'[33]

All these comments need to be seen in conjunction with Pierre's well-known ability to listen carefully to others, to work well with them and to inspire them. The same François Chavancs, speaking about Pierre's time as director of the diocesan pastoral and study centre, *Les Glycines,* says: 'It was then that Pierre showed great qualities: contradictory qualities rarely to be found in the same person. He possessed a natural authority, an assurance in his judgements. He showed an energy and a determination in his work and at the same time a great capacity for listening.... With everyone, Pierre maintained a personal relationship. Through his welcoming attitude, his public statements [and] as animator of its varied activities he fostered a spirit of unity in the centre.' [34]

DIDN'T FOLLOW THE CROWD

When I asked people who knew Pierre well how they viewed his independent mind-set, their answers were very similar. Mgr Teissier noted that he, as Archbishop and President of the Episcopal Conference, had worked closely with Pierre. He always found him easy to work with: 'We often produced papers together and we had no differences. ... There never was any friction in our relations.' [35] Mgr Claude Rault wrote: 'It's a fact that Pierre was endowed with a very strong personality, with a rather steely temperament. Stubborn? Yes, he was obstinate. But he was so more by personal, enlightened conviction. He wasn't a person to follow the crowd, but went before it on dangerous paths ... and knew how to take risks himself without imposing them on others.' And Jean-Jacques Pérennès had this to say: 'To be stubborn is a failing if one remains obstinate when one is mistaken. This wasn't true in his case. He was stubborn, convinced that great things take time to ripen.'

As regards his relationship with Cardinal Duval people are also in agreement. Jean-Jacques Pérennès writes: 'The tensions with Mgr Duval arose from the fact that they came from two very different religious worlds and from two very different generations, but at the same time Pierre had an enormous admiration for Cardinal Duval, who was worthy of it and he too [the Cardinal], was a courageous man, and "stubborn" or obstinate in the dark hours of the Algerian war. Having said that, the Cardinal was a man of the past, very rigid regarding ecclesiastical discipline (priests' dress, etc.), while at the same time very farsighted and even visionary in political matters.' Pierre's sister Anne-Marie made a shrewd observation: 'As regards Mgr Duval, you must remember that Pierre's youth was immersed in the *pieds-noirs* milieu which mostly saw the Cardinal as a traitor and, as well, Pierre was embarrassed by the Cardinal's attachment to the traditions and pomp of the liturgy, but Mgr Duval knew how to tame Pierre!'

Some might see Pierre's refusal to budge on matters of principle as a sign of stubbornness and disobedience; to Pierre and others it was a sign of personal integrity. And it was precisely on account of what Pierre saw to be 'the needs of the mission' that he resisted his transfer to Egypt and to France. And as the future would show, he was to remain courageously faithful to his Christian principles, even at the cost of his life.

6

Leaving One's Whole World Behind

AFTER reading in 1970 a biography, *Histoire de ma vie*, by Fadhma
Amrouche, a Kabyle Christian, Pierre reflected on the Church's
inability before independence to appreciate and understand Algerian society. He commented (and this comment reflects Pierre's own
valiant efforts at enculturation in an independent Algeria): 'If only
from time to time we could see the world through the eyes of the
other person (as far as possible), we would avoid so many stupidi-
ties. It is the first condition of respect to accept to leave one's own
world behind, however perfect it may appear to us to be, to enter
into communion with the other's truth: and that we haven't done
and continue not to do.' [1]

Pierre was well aware of the need for self-knowledge and spiritual
insight. In one of his final retreats he declared that a lack of spiritual
insight 'brings in its train all kinds of disorder, because we cannot
see clearly. As for me, [spiritual] blindness terrifies me interiorly
more than the terrorists.' [2] When Pierre became aware of the effect
his own behaviour was having on others, when they reacted, for example, very aggressively, he scrutinised himself in order to see in
what way he might have provoked this unexpected reaction. Lack of
spiritual insight, says Pierre, makes us mistake evil for good and is
at the root of all disorder: 'My constant prayer is to see clearly.' [3] To
understand oneself clearly, to be self-aware, is part of the newness
of life given by the Spirit. Here Pierre is one with all the spiritual

masters who teach us that the first step on the way to conversion is
to recognise that we are sinners.

The challenge of seeing issues through the eyes of the other came
home to Pierre in a rather brutal manner. In the summer of 1969 he
started teaching Arabic to French-speaking Algerians who wished to
acquire a mastery of written Arabic. In his very first class he discovered that his students included a woman who had planted a bomb
in a bar in the centre of Algiers during the war of independence.
In the ensuing explosion some of his friends had been mutilated
and injured: 'I admit that at that instant my stomach tensed and I
struggled. And then, in getting to know her better, I discovered the
reasons which had led her to commit that act. Well, I found out that
in fact we were very similar. If I had been immersed in a comparable
situation I don't think I would have gone so far as to commit an act
like that but at any rate I would have better understood what impelled those people to act as they did.' [4]

Psychological and spiritual growth demand, says Pierre, that we
leave ourselves behind, that we risk taking a step into the unknown.
Taking the risk to leave our securities behind leads to new life and is
the principle which governs our human and spiritual development:
'To leave oneself behind is the only way to life.' [5] And this was the
challenge which Pierre sought to take up as he gave himself whole-
heartedly to his vocation of being Christ's presence to his Algerian
brothers and sisters. Writing to his parents in December, 1967, he
observed that Algerians couldn't afford to take an annual holiday
as he did: 'I think one must know how to share a little the living
conditions of our brothers in this country: personally I would like to
do so more but for the moment one mustn't try to do everything. I'll
take on later the life of those to whom I will be sent; at present I'm
in a state of transition. I know that I will never be completely one of
them but I'll become so in as far as the Lord gives me the strength.' [6]
As his Arabic improved Pierre rejoiced in the fact that he was gradually beginning to make friendships with Algerians and beginning to

enter their world: 'It's a case of finding a way in to their world by any means possible and learning to open one's heart and one's eyes. The rest will come about in God's good time.'[7] All of these efforts were inspired by his 'conversion experience', his dawning awareness of the barriers which the European settlers and the Church had erected in order to preserve their privileged status.

LOVE AT FIRST SIGHT

The Arabisation of the country gathered speed as the newly independent nation sought to shake off the language and the Christian culture of its former colonial ruler. Pierre devoted a huge amount of time to learning Arabic and immersing himself in the Algerian way of life as he realised that without this immersion he would never make much progress in understanding the Algerian mentality and outlook on life.

The key people in helping him master Arabic were the Lebanese sisters of The Holy Hearts of Jesus and Mary (Les Saints Coeurs de Jésus et de Marie), a religious congregation founded by the Jesuits in the middle of the nineteenth century to educate Lebanese women. The sisters were highly educated and dynamic. The Algerians were bowled over by them and amazed when they discovered that they were Christians. They spoke better Arabic than the Algerians and had a relaxed relationship with both sexes which, at that time, was unusual for women in Algeria. Pierre was enchanted by their competence and zest for life. He admired their ability to witness to the Gospel without attempting to proselytise. He wrote to his father: 'No proselytism in their attitude but a love and a true disinterested service of the people to whom they are sent.... And I continue to think that only Arabs can really evangelise Arabs. Coming from the Middle East they are, moreover, crowned with a prestige which we can't imagine.'[8] The admiration was mutual. The sisters admired Pierre's devotion to learning the language and his rapid progress.

They also admired his spirituality and devotion to prayer. He frequently celebrated Mass for them in Arabic and the sisters invited him to give retreats in Lebanon. He struck up a strong friendship with the superior, Sr Athina Fadel, who would describe Pierre as her 'son'.[9] Sr Athina provided Pierre with both the inspiration and admiration which he needed to pursue so tenaciously his enculturation into the Arab world.

Various comments in his letters indicate a growing identification with the independent Algeria: 'I return to Alger by road to-morrow. My country is truly splendid.'[10] And in July 1968 Pierre writes: 'One must at all costs penetrate a little the language to begin to appreciate the gulf which separates us: truly the Algerian affair [war of independence] was absolutely inevitable and the future is still not clear as regards our relations with the western countries. I confess that it's beginning to be love at first sight (a very gradual love at first sight...) with the language and the Arab world.'[11]

Pierre made a conscious effort not to be sucked into the embassy cocktail circuit though he did establish a close friendship with the Pakistani ambassador whom he met frequently for meals which often lasted until midnight. However, he systematically avoided functions at the French embassy as, presumably, he didn't wish to identify the Algerian Church with the French colonial past. In fact, he tells his father that the first time he entered the French embassy was on 15 March 1980 to have lunch with André Miquel, a visiting French Islamologist.

TOO MANY AMBIGUITIES

To be an Algerian was *ipso facto* to be Muslim. Pierre comments that it was, and is, possible to hold Algerian citizenship without being Muslim but such a person is regarded as not being fully Algerian. Algeria, in the past, practised an open and welcoming Islam. However, with the politicisation of Islam, Pierre notes that its expression had now become more doctrinaire and less open. In the 1980s the single-party socialist state found itself caught in the paradoxical situation of having to promote socialism and Islam at the same time: 'The state then found itself involved in an ambiguous politics: economically and socially "socialist", culturally "Arab-Islamic". Each new advance of socialism (the agricultural revolution, state monopoly of education...) had to have its Islamic counterpart (moving the week-end to Friday, religious education in the schools, family law).'[12]

The progressive Arabisation of the country brought home to Pierre the increasing difficulty of maintaining the institutional structures of the Church and its cultural identity. In December 1971 he wrote that for the first time since independence all outward signs of Christmas had been abolished – no Christmas decorations in the street or in the shops. Any Christmas advertising had to state that it only concerned 'foreigners and Algerians who are Christians'. The emphasis would now be on celebrating the birth of the Prophet and on the two great Muslim feasts.[13]

In December 1974 he commented on the crisis facing the diocesan schools which were being obliged by a government decree to raise teachers' salaries by 30 per cent. He noted that the schools hadn't got the resources to pay for such a rise: 'I think that all of this will hasten the end of Church works. And it isn't a bad thing, in one sense, because they carry too many ambiguities (the propagation of French culture, selection on financial grounds, the formation of a privileged class...).'[14] Pierre's comments would prove to be prophetic. All the Catholic schools and hospitals were nationalised in 1976. This had the unexpected result of bringing the Church, bereft of institutional power, closer to the people and especially to the more deprived sectors of Algerian society.

A letter dated 14 October 1975 ends on a note of foreboding as Pierre announces to his parents that the army had taken over the iconic church building of Notre-Dame d'Afrique on the spurious grounds of installing an antenna on the roof. At the same time the Basilica of Santa Cruz in Oran and St Augustine's Basilica in Annaba were likewise occupied.[15] As regards Santa Cruz in Oran, Pierre commented that it was too visible and too imposing for the 'mini-Church' of Algeria to hold on to. Happily, his prognostic in this regard hasn't come to pass and in March 2017 this basilica was renovated and restored to its former glory.

In the same letter he makes an insightful comment about the psychology of the Algerian people. Europeans who continued to live in Algeria were often frustrated by the disorder which reigned in public administration. However, Pierre thinks that their discouragement arises from 'expecting too much, too soon. A people does not evolve at the rhythm, already slow, of individuals. And, moreover, the more this people really gains stability, the more it becomes conscious of its personality and the more it becomes worried about its dignity before others. The present phase is about self-affirmation. Let's hope that the phase of relating confidently (which presumes self-confidence) will finally arrive. But in the meantime one must hold on.'[16] This insight has proved to be particularly true as Algeria and France have stumbled in their relationship from misunderstanding to misunderstanding.[17]

A CHURCH STRIPPED OF INSTITUTIONAL POWER

In the third volume of his letters, *La où se posent les vraies questions, 1975-1981* (*There where the real questions are asked, 1975-1981*) this same theme of the diminishment of the institutional Church continues. He arrived back in Algiers from Rome on June 24, 1976 to find that the *Glycines'* library has been closed and sealed by the police. The publication of the *Revue de presse,* a monthly compendium of North African newspaper articles, and the *Revue des Revues* had also been forbidden as was the teaching of Arabic. After much negotiation the library was allowed to re-open and the magazines to continue. And the study centre was once more given permission to teach Arabic to foreigners, but not to Algerians.

Meanwhile, in July 1976 Mgr Jacquier, the auxiliary bishop of Algiers, had been murdered in the street, apparently by a mentally disturbed man, and in August of the same year Pierre's great friends, the Lebanese sisters, had their apartment requisitioned by the state. In July 1977 Pierre noted that 12 priests had left the archdiocese of Algiers, seven the diocese of Oran and one or two the diocese of Constantine and Hippone, all, presumably, having chosen to move to French dioceses. And to further drive home the realisation that Algeria was becoming a more inhospitable environment for the small Christian remnant, Sunday August 22 1976 was the last Sunday to be kept as a public holiday; from then on Friday would become the official day of rest. In the same year the Church schools and hospitals were nationalised, although I can find no mention of this momentous event in Pierre's letters. One can feel the noose tightening on the institutional life of the Church, although Pierre, buoyed up by his many Algerian contacts and relationships, does not appear to be unduly worried by these developments.

Another reminder of the diminishing numbers and influence of the Christian presence surfaced at the start of Pierre's episcopal ministry in Oran. Questions were raised about the continuing use of the Sacred Heart Cathedral by the much reduced Catholic community. The cathedral was in fact the property of the State and various Muslim groups were expressing an interest in obtaining it for use as a mosque. As the cathedral was too big for the small number of worshippers and there was the danger that it might be occupied by Islamists, Pierre handed it over in May 1983 to the Minister for Culture, M. Abdelmajid Meziane, who subsequently converted it into a library and a cultural centre. In return the local authorities agreed to Pierre's request for some financial compensation in order to transform the parish church of Saint-Eugène into a modest replacement cathedral. Thanks to Pierre's sensitivity to local feeling, and the sympathetic response of the local authorities and the Minister for Culture, this potentially divisive issue was resolved amicably.[18]

Writing in his diocesan magazine, *Le Lien*, June-July 1990, Pierre reflected on the demise of the institutional structures of the Church:

> We, the little Church in Algeria, can testify that up until now nothing has been lost by becoming poorer and simpler. Our fears about losing our works, our property, our influence have given way to confidence. For we have gained in humanity and in intensity from what we have had to leave behind. Fraternity, simplicity, openness: everyone now tries to live these out through sharing and service. Through work we contribute to the wellbeing of the country in a number of significant sections of the economy or of the social sector (education, health). Through our involvement in voluntary organisations, we collaborate in the care of the deprived. And all of that without any patronising claims of 'showing charity', or imposing our presence or services, but simply by contributing constructively to the society where we find ourselves as a result of birth, vocation or volunteering overseas.[19]

As bishop of the diocese of Oran, Pierre presided over a dying Church community. With the growing influence of Islamism and fewer overseas aid workers (*coopérants*), the number of Christians was diminishing. It had also become more difficult for non-Algerian citizens to find work in state institutions. The Church responded by setting up meeting places for service and encounter, what Pierre called '*plates-formes de service et de rencontre*', where the religious sisters and Catholic aid workers could meet with and serve the local community. Thus libraries for students, centres for the handicapped, and for female formation were set up and continue to this day.

NOT SATAN PERSONIFIED

In July 1989 Pierre gave a conference to the Dominican sisters of the Presentation of Tours[20] outlining the history of the Church in Algeria. One negative legacy of the colonial period was that Algerians saw the Christian as the coloniser, the person who had come to occupy his country, the Frenchman. Pierre, however, qualifies this negative image by pointing out that many religious communities, before independence, were at the service of the Muslim community. On the Algerian national stage the one-party socialist experiment had failed, the western model of capitalism, symbolic of the coloniser, was rejected and this left only one other option, a return to their origins, the Islamic solution.

The Church had, observed Pierre, an important mission: not to proselytise but firstly to evangelise, that is to show freely God's love for every person, to move out of their 'bubbles', 'to go towards others and to create with others covenants of peace, covenants of friendships ... a covenantal and reconciling Church.'[21] The second and third part of her mission in Algeria were to welcome new Christians and to engage in interreligious dialogue. Pierre sums up his vision of a diminishing Christian presence in Algeria as follows:

> So, the first mission: covenant, reconciliation with the Muslim world such as it is; the second mission: to welcome and accompany those who discover Jesus Christ. And the third mission: interreligious dialogue.... Thus, *it is imperative that the Church be present in the Muslim world*, despite all the suffering which this may involve for those who find themselves in this position, so that from within the Muslim world *she may make known the face of Jesus Christ*! By living the Gospel in the Muslim world Muslims will come to know Christians not solely on the basis of their reputation, or of history but through a Christian life and a Christian witness. This witness is important in modifying the Muslim judgement of Christians. Robust

Christians are needed, even if few in number, to be a symbolic but steadfast presence. Thus Muslims can say: 'What you say about Christians isn't true; we have met some ... and they aren't Satan personified!' '[22]

7

Taking the Side of the Powerless

A CHURCH stripped of its institutional power was congenial to
Pierre's way of thinking. A theme which we will meet again and
again in his writing and preaching is the need for the Church to be
present in people's lives at the points of suffering and exclusion, the
place of the Cross where Jesus unambiguously took the side of the
powerless and became one with them in his death outside the camp,
outside the city walls. He called these privileged places of witness
to Christ 'the fault lines' of suffering humanity, *les lignes de fracture*:
'The Church's place is ... on all these fault lines, between human
groups and inside each human being, everywhere where there are
wounded, excluded, marginalised people. We are well and truly
here [in Algeria] in our place.'[1] Pierre wrote in 1994 that the Cross
is the bridge between God and man:

> He [Jesus] opened his arms to stretch out between his ene-
> mies the bridge of reconciliation. The sign of the cross, which
> appears blasphemous to so many [Muslim] believers, is for
> us the link between God and humanity and between human
> beings. This cross carries a brutalised man who gives his life,
> rather than take it from others, to bring about God's plan.[2]

And it is the Church's glory to be Jesus' reconciling presence in our
violent and broken world.

SOLIDARITY WITH THE EXCLUDED

If we wish to enter into communion with others or with Christ, writes Pierre, we too have to offer ourselves in a real manner like Jesus, to enter into Jesus' Passover from death to life – his offering of himself on our behalf – so that the forces of death might be overcome: 'Our solidarity, our incarnation, our presence are after the manner of Jesus.'[3] Pierre explains that Jesus' offering has two complementary aspects. First of all, we see a God who refused to have anything to do with 'violence, lies, power and domination: he is nothing except love. He can do nothing against violence and domination except to allow himself to be crucified. He invites me to take no part in the game of violence and domination.'[4] Secondly, Jesus in his self-offering takes the side of the powerless and little ones, showing the face of a God who is not with the self-important and wealthy of this world. We too are called to offer our lives in a concrete manner in the struggle against the forces of death: 'It is in this way that we make ourselves present to Christ; by uprooting our egos, the presence of Christ becomes real in us. It is also in this way that our communion has a chance of existing, our communion with each other, when each one tries to give their life for their friends.'[5]

And Jesus lived in the middle of suffering and distress, in the midst of a suffering humanity, a solidarity which led him to the Cross. That is likewise the mission of the Church, to be Jesus' reconciling presence in places of suffering and distress:

> The place of Christians is there where humanity is broken, whether it be people who are inwardly broken as a result of sickness, exclusion, life's difficulties; whether it be between human groups who exclude each other; whether it be between peoples or between great religions which have been in conflict from the beginning; we are positioned there on these fault lines and in a way trying to keep hold of both realities, strongly believing that, through the love which God gives us to live,

reconciliation is possible. On these fault lines of the world, in the cause of reconciliation, that is the place of the Church. If she isn't there, she is nowhere.[6]

Throughout the family correspondence Pierre reveals unequivocally his preferential option for the marginalised and weak. He is acutely aware of their powerlessness when faced by the political intrigues of the powerful who wish to use them for their own material advantage.

The inability of many of the *pieds-noirs*, now in exile, to understand the poverty and inequality which the Algerians experienced during French rule pains him. In December 1972, reflecting on the ministry of Fr Lefèvre, the Dominican chaplain to the scouts in pre-independence Algiers, he is brought up against the paradox that a person can be very generous and selfless in personal relationships and yet blind to the political and structural consequences of the institutions which they support. Therein lies the issue of the Church's participation in colonialism: 'We can't rest content with a personal morality, however admirable it may be; we can be the most devoted of people [like Fr Lefèvre] and the most selfless and the most charitable and everything imaginable, and be at the same time the instruments of the most terrible exploitation. The missionaries ought to know this, they who have served, without distinction, the cross and the flag.'[7]

THE ROOTS OF VIOLENCE

This general indifference to the suffering of the poor and powerless, according to Pierre, extends beyond colonial Algeria to all of the developed countries which are only interested, for the most part, in their own prosperity and security. Pierre commented in January 1970 on the ending of the war in Biafra: 'The imposing silence of the great powers before these millions of dead who were killing each other with our arms and with the help of our "technical" advisors, while everyone is talking about Vietnam where the losses are a hundred times smaller ... but where the Americans are directly involved – or about the Middle East where the losses are even smaller but where we are all directly concerned ... this silence is the sign of our profound indifference to everything which does not impinge directly on our lives.'[8]

And Pierre makes a similar point in November 1974 when reflecting on strikes in France and the political deals of the big oil companies in order to control the market price of petrol. The blame for the strikes and prices will always be passed on to those unable to defend themselves. And if this unjust set-up leads to violence, people will react indignantly: 'Taking all this into account, I prefer systematically to take the side of the powerless, even if their arguments are doubtful and their means of defence "incorrect"; they are less brutal than the deals and the means of pressure used by the powerful, and their struggle is a struggle for life.'[9]

Reacting in September 1972 to the killing of Israeli Olympic athletes in Munich by the Palestinians, Pierre reflects on the inconsistency of public opinion. It is quick to condemn desperate, one-off acts of violence by people who have been ignored by politicians and who are left with no other means of making themselves heard: 'We reacted in exactly the same way when Algerians, in murderous attacks, started the Algerian war: how many futile attempts at conciliation, how many futile undertakings, how many disappointed hopes, how many broken promises, how many humiliations suffered, how many injustices were at the root of this "violence".'[10] In these occasional comments in his letters home, we can see Pierre's acute sense of justice and sensitivity towards the underdog. His sensibility has been all the more refined by his own experience of seeing life from the other side of the fence, the side of the 'good' colonialist, the Fr Lefèvres of this world. To understand the life of the underdog, he observes, requires an openness of heart to people who are different.

In a retreat given in July 1983 Pierre, now Bishop of Oran, reflected on the *pied-noir* experience of being separated from the Muslim *other*, of living in a ghetto. Here he shares with us his mature thinking about the 'original sin' which would prove to be the eventual downfall of the *pieds-noirs*. The great temptation for all minorities, he thinks, is to seek to protect their own existence by cutting themselves off from those who are different. To do this, Pierre affirms, is to seek death. The great truth of our faith is that to find life we need to leave ourselves behind, to go out of ourselves rather than building protective walls around ourselves. It is, paradoxically, by leaving ourselves behind that we strengthen our identity: 'It's in the search for the other that one is reborn. It is in communion with the one who is different that one accedes to a more fruitful life.'[11] We may suffer some wounds in the process but these too can be a source of new life. Our vulnerability can make us fruitful: 'In any case our only missionary ambition in Muslim countries ... I believe, is to make contact with a people so that by this contact God can, when he so wishes, transmit his Spirit.'[12]

In April 2017 I started talking at a bus stop in Toulouse (it's a friendly city!) to a former *pied-noir* lady on her way home from daily Mass. When I asked her if she had ever gone back to visit Alger, her home town, she replied: 'No, it would be too painful. All my beautiful memories would be ruined. The Arabs don't know how to look after the environment. It was we who reclaimed the land.' This woman was a practising Catholic, and no doubt a wonderful person, yet she couldn't put herself in the place of those who suffered under the colonial presence. She couldn't see things from the other person's, the underdog's point of view. And therein lay the whole tragedy of the Algerian war of independence.

TO BREAK THROUGH SOME MORE BARRIERS

Pierre's commitment to working for justice was not confined to his writing and preaching. He was also involved at a practical level through his work for *Rencontre et Développement* (*Encounter and Development*). In this development agency run by the Algerian Protestant Church he was unanimously elected president in November 1976.

In the 1970s Algeria, a country which had successfully thrown off the shackles of colonial rule, wished to be seen as a leader of the developing nations. Many of the exiled leaders from countries such as Angola and Mozambique, then fighting for independence, were given refuge in Algiers. Pierre, who, according to his friend Jean-Jacques Pérennès,[13] had no taste for political action, did what he could to support these exiles and their political struggle. In May 1980 he commented that now that these developing countries had, for the most part, gained political independence 'two important problems hold our attention: neo-colonialism and emigration, in other words the new relationships established between countries. As well as these, there are the relationships with those who are still fighting to have their voices and their rights acknowledged: the Palestinians and the Sahraouis.'[14] In March 1980, for example, Pierre, in his capacity as president of *Rencontre et Développement,* was trying to help young French Algerians to gain the right to re-enter France after having been expelled for minor infractions of the law.

In his farewell letter, on being appointed Bishop of Oran, to his brothers in the Dominican Order, he neatly summarises the wide-ranging commitments which this work entailed: 'In 1974, thanks to Pastor Blanc, I took up a serious commitment in a branch of the CIMADE [15] in Algiers, which became *Rencontre et Développement*. It's there, on the job and through a series of practical interventions, that I did my apprenticeship learning about the universal and political dimension of Algerian problems. Support for the liberation movements (Palestine, Africa, Sahara), reflecting on development and neo-colonialism in our countries, the fight for the recognition of the elementary rights of emigrants (in which the Algiers brothers

took part), an aid programme for the Sahraouis refugees or participation in the reconstruction of El Asnam [destroyed by an earth-
quake]: all of those activities were undertaken in common with militants from many countries and various ideological backgrounds. I
was thus enabled to break through some more barriers and to better
understand what was at stake in the struggles and hopes of other
peoples.' [16]

A NEW AND LIFE-GIVING WAY

In 1989 Pierre described the mission of the tiny Christian Church in
Algeria, in the sea of Islam, as one of reconciliation. Everything separated the two faiths: there were huge doctrinal differences, painful
historical memories and growing divisions between Christians and
Muslims in many parts of the world. The Church in Algeria operated from a position of vulnerability and weakness. She lived on the
margins and had no institutional power to wield. Being human,
comments Pierre, she would have liked to be less marginalised, less
humiliated, less despised.

Paradoxically, it was from this position of powerlessness that
they were best able to carry out their mission of reconciliation. People weren't afraid of them and in this position of vulnerability there
was an opportunity, Pierre thought, to make a new friendship, a new
covenant with Algerian Muslims, one that wasn't based on the usual
power struggle between Christians and Muslims: 'The mission of
reconciliation works through poverty. And I repeat: believe you me
it's not easy, pride takes a terrible knock! Being in the Muslim world
is really an intense experience for us.' [17] The only riches which the
Church now possessed, having been stripped of her institutional
power, were human relationships. And in her poverty she was able
to reach out to others in a new and life-giving way.

This reaching out was tested to the full when the country suc-
cumbed to the violence of a brutal civil war. Should the small re-

maining Christian community, mainly composed of non-nationals, pack up its bags and shake the dust off their feet? Pierre's commitment to his suffering compatriots was expressed clearly in one of his last conferences given in Grenoble in April 1996. People outside Algeria often asked him why he continued to remain in the country, given the tiny number of Christians and the violence to which they were exposed. Pierre replied that they had lived moments of great exaltation with the Muslim people of Algeria in the past but now a time of suffering, violence and sorrow had arrived. On account of their covenant of solidarity with the people they had no choice but to remain faithful to them: 'One doesn't abandon one's own when they are suffering.' [18]

They aren't like aid workers who move on when times become dangerous and there are other projects to attend to: 'We are bound to a people, bound by friendship and bound by all the solidarities of daily life, bound in suffering as we were bound in hope, in joy. Everything we do, everything we live is measured in terms of relationships to be made, to keep alive, to deepen with this people in whose midst we find ourselves.' [19] And having put his hand to the plough in imitation of his divine Master, Pierre, out of love, refused to turn back.

8

Confronting the Powers of Darkness

THE CAUSES of the Algerian civil war were many but the main ones included the rise of Islamism, the inevitable corruption caused by the single-party rule of the National Liberation Front (FLN) from 1962 to 1988, and the failure of the economy to provide employment and adequate housing for a rapidly expanding population. In the light of the political corruption and the serious social problems, the people, especially the young, looked to the rising tide of the Islamic movement to provide a way out. The cancellation by the military-backed junta of the second round of elections in 1992, because the Islamists were assured of a crushing victory, led to the outbreak of the civil war.

What people hadn't foreseen, however, was the pitiless nature of the ensuing armed struggle between the Islamists and the government. The extent of the callous violence and contempt for moral values which the civilian population, and the tiny Christian minority, had to endure during the black decade, the *décennie noire* of 1992-2002 beggars the imagination. The Armed Islamic Group (GIA) raped, tortured and murdered innocent men, women and children, sincerely believing that they were serving God; and the government security forces retaliated in a similar pitiless manner.

The GIA quickly began to target, not only the police and military, but also intellectuals, journalists, artists, imams, foreigners. As the cities became more secure, attacks were directed at the poor

in isolated villages and unprotected suburbs. The civilian population became the victims of fake roadblocks, car bombs, massacres.
In 1997-98 the GIA guerrillas began to massacre entire villages and
neighbourhoods, killing, on some occasions, hundreds of innocent
civilians regardless of age or sex. Anyone not supporting the GIA
was considered to be an apostate and hence subject to the death
penalty: 'The Raïs and Bentalha massacres in particular shocked
world-wide observers. Pregnant women were sliced open, children
were hacked to pieces or dashed against walls, men's limbs were
hacked off one by one, and, as the attackers retreated, they would
kidnap young women to keep as sex slaves.'[1]

The violence and terror experienced by the Algerian people, and
by Pierre and the tiny Christian community, was the violence of a
civil war. The enemy couldn't be clearly seen or delineated. Pierre
commented: 'Death can come from anywhere, anytime and from
anyone.'[2] The security forces couldn't be easily distinguished from
the GIA as they were often in plain clothes and unmarked cars
whereas the Islamists dressed up in police and army uniforms and
set up fake roadblocks. Excesses on both sides led to further reprisals and an escalation of violence: 'All means are then considered
acceptable and the worst are the most effective. We watch power-
lessly the martyrdom of a people who no longer knows whom it can
trust.'[3]

SPEAKING THE TRUTH

In the last few years of his life Pierre became more and more outspo-
ken. In his editorials in *Le Lien*, the diocesan magazine published ten
times a year, his criticism of Islamic fundamentalism – its violence
and manipulative use of religion for political ends – became more
and more scathing. In the October 1993 issue Pierre reported that
an estimated 370 people had been killed since the beginning of the
summer in the growing violence, among them the first two foreign-

ers, François Thélet and Emmanuel Didion from the Sidi Bel Abbès area of his diocese. Of course, he was aware that his outspokenness would have personal consequences, the most likely outcome being his assassination.

What was Pierre's approach to the Islamists? He believed in talking to people who held different viewpoints from his own but he didn't think it wise to negotiate politically with people who were still determined to use force in order to achieve their ends, namely the setting up of an Islamic state. In the January 1992 issue of *Le Lien* [4] he wrote about his stance *vis-à-vis* the Islamic Salvation Front (FIS) and its stated objective of setting up an Islamic state in Algeria. The FIS, he claimed, would, in the medium term, repudiate the democratic process in which it had earlier participated in an attempt to gain power. It would impose 'the judgement of God which brooks no opposition.... I expect nothing good to come from any religious power, Jewish, Christian or Muslim. I still have confidence in the Algerian people, even in some of those who are hoping for an Islamic solution. We are not in Iran, nor in the Sudan nor in Saudi Arabia. I am in favour of democracy (whose limitations I recognise) and of respect for human rights. I will support then, with the caution imposed by "our Christian difference", those who will defend it.' [5]

Pierre did believe in dialogue but he didn't believe in giving respectability to a political organisation and its armed wing, the GIA, which had little respect for democratic processes. The FIS was prepared to use the most barbaric means to achieve their goal of an Islamic state, all in the name of God. In an editorial in the June-July 1991 issue of *Le Lien* he succinctly summarised the Islamist attitude towards democracy: 'Essentially there can be no question of submitting the divine law to the vagaries of the majority. The very principle of democracy is foreign to this religious conception of power because it [democracy] assumes a clear distinction between power and religion.' [6]

RESISTING THE SURROUNDING VIOLENCE

In his 1994 Christmas letter Pierre spoke about the support he was receiving from Christians who had decided to remain and likewise the support he was receiving from his Algerian friends, known and unknown. This solidarity in suffering gave him strength and hope: 'This young man at the market offers a rose to a sister saying: "It's the rose of friendship; the Algerian people aren't mean". This faithful friend who telephones and often calls by to make sure that everything is well and offers his help or simply shares his worries. For these and many others, I'll remain. I even find a real happiness in remaining ... make of it what you will.'[7]

All of this mayhem wasn't permanent, but only episodic. Pierre noted that life continued more or less as normal with people attending prudently to their daily routines. The shops were well stocked although the high prices reflected the economic crisis. The public services – hospitals, schools, universities – functioned as best they could despite being hampered by budgetary restrictions, the brain drain and the ambient violence. By continuing to lead as normal a life as possible, the people showed their defiance of the terrorists: 'With them, militants and intellectuals express in the press their resistance to violence, at the cost of their lives. They are looking for ways of finding a political solution and leading a daily struggle against passivity, resignation, discouragement, injustice, marginalization, exclusion, the arrogance of the rich and powerful, the contempt towards little ones and the poor, the perversion of religion ... Saïd Mekbel[8] was one of these and he isn't the only one.'[9] Pierre, undoubtedly, felt a great affinity with these Algerians who courageously opposed the obscurantism of the Islamists and whose bravery and integrity gave him hope for a better future.

In his editorials Pierre speaks openly and courageously about the challenges and suffering of witnessing to the Gospel in the bitter climate of a civil war in which the few remaining Christians have become pawns. He knows that he will most likely suffer the fate of the other religious who have been assassinated. There was also, one senses in his editorials and other conferences, a fluctuating mood. On the one hand, he was moved and grateful for the powerful personal support which he was receiving from his many Muslim friends and, on the other hand, there was, at times, a hint of despair and hopelessness brought on by the bigotry and sectarian mentality of the extremists.

One can sense in the background his perplexity and questioning of his own fidelity to the Algerian nation. Has his life's work for reconciliation and inclusion been a dream? Does he really belong in Algeria? Sometimes in his talks and writings he refers to 'my country' and at other times he speaks of himself as a foreigner.

A MORE INTENSE TASTE FOR LIVING

In a moving and intense editorial in the June-July 1994 issue of *Le Lien*,[10] 'Pray unceasingly' (*Priez sans cesse*) Pierre describes the disillusion and the difficulties which threaten the Christian community in a war-torn and intolerant Algeria. All their work for mutual understanding, respect and dialogue between the two communities appears to be threatened by the rise of an intolerant Islam. And now they are accused of 'being infidels, or believers in bad faith because we refuse to become Muslims or, worse still, of being new crusaders suspected of wishing to destroy Islam from within. How can one not become hardened in the face of such accusations...'.

In addition, those Christians choosing to remain in Algeria are experiencing pressures from family and religious superiors to reconsider their decision. And perhaps the cruellest blow of all is the decision by some of the religious congregations, traditionally supporters of the Algerian Church, to withdraw their personnel for reasons which aren't entirely clear, saying: 'We are forced to leave you in midstream. You will have to continue the crossing without us.'[11]

Faced by all of these too human doubts, Pierre reminds his readers of the nature of the God whom they serve: 'Jesus tells us and
proves to us that God is passionate, that Love is his name. In his
attitude and in his teaching he is always transgressing the cold logic
of the Law and of Reason.... What could be crazier than to go to face
death without any defence other than a disarmed and disarming
love which dies while forgiving? ... We, however, belong to that race
of believers.' Pierre goes on to say that they are invited to leave behind the 'wisdom of the Greeks' and embrace the 'folly of the Cross',
opening themselves to the power of the Spirit: 'Now our life gets its
flavour and fecundity when it runs the risk of that distinctive folly
which permeates the Gospel with a jubilant audacity.'

Confronted by so many risks and disillusionments, Christians
need, more than ever, to pray and open their hearts to the transforming presence of Jesus: 'This moment of crisis, of trial, of distur-
bance, is perhaps an unique opportunity to allow God to touch you
and to find, with Jesus and through Jesus, a more intense taste for
living and loving, an inner necessity which imposes itself when one
has lost one's certainties, one's defences, and one's pitiful means.'[12]

THE UNQUENCHABLE FIRE OF GOD'S LOVE

The indiscriminate killing and terror which was being inflicted on
so many innocent Algerians struck the tiny Christian community
for the first time on 8 May 1994 when Br Henri and Sr Paul-Hélène
were gunned down as they went about their work of helping students in the Kasbah, a poor district of Algiers. Pierre was unable
to contain his anger at the cowardice and depravity of their killers.
He expressed his indignation and disbelief in the May 1994 editorial of *Le Lien*, '*Pourquoi?*' ('Why?'). His first sentence sets the tone:
'We knew well that some people considered us to be dangerous and
baneful beings, the aftermath of a colonial past, agents manipulated
by a cultural neo-colonialism, implacable enemies of Islam, set on

destroying it from within...' [13] Pierre went on to outline the educational, humanitarian and cultural work which was undertaken by Christians in Algeria, a work which sought to help Algerians assume their full humanity and cultural identity. This work was carried out without any attempt whatsoever to proselytise but merely to enable Christians and Muslims better appreciate each other.

In the context of this sharing of a common humanity Pierre cannot restrain his righteous anger at the mindless violence of the Islamists:

And what abominable cowardice is shown by these shadowy killers! That I should be targeted is understandable: as a bishop, I represent, perhaps in the eyes of some, a despised and dangerous institution. I am a leader and I have always defended publicly whatever has appeared to me to be just, true, all that promotes freedom, respect for people, especially the vulnerable and those in a minority. I have worked tirelessly for dialogue and friendship among peoples, cultures and religions. All of that has probably merited for me death and I am willing to run the risk. It would even be a tribute which I would pay to God in whom I believe. But to take it out on Br Henri and Sr Paul-Hélène, that I cannot understand.[14]

Having expressed his emotions, Pierre seeks to understand what has happened, to get at the deeper reasons for these killings and the real people responsible for them:

We do not cry out for vengeance. We are the unwitting and unfortunate witnesses of depravities brought about by decades of poor management, by the manipulation and political exploitation of culture and religion. Those who carry out these crimes against humanity do not know what they are doing, as Jesus said about the torturers who were crucifying him, and he added: Father, forgive them! The guilty ones are those who have created the conditions for this dehumanisation and who have supplied its ideological justification. We can only entrust ourselves to Him while continuing with our mission.[15]

Pierre reacted again with horror and anger in an editorial, 'Bravo!', in *Le Lien*, November 1995, to the assassination of Sr Odette and the wounding of Sr Chantal on 6 November in Algiers. His contempt for the cowardly assassins was made clear. Each of the six sections of the editorial starts with an ironic 'Bravo!', the opening sentence being: 'Bravo! The heroic combatants of justice have struck again.... Bravo! To you who have chosen this kind of war which you sometimes call *djihad*, a holy war against the enemies of God, the tyrants, the corrupt and the hypocrites, "the infidels, the Jews and the Christians" (GIA *dixit*).'[16] With each successive 'Bravo' Pierre challenges the lies and half-truths which are being proclaimed in Algeria by the men of violence. For Pierre, the end does not justify the means; people are not merely expendable pawns in a political struggle. As a follower of Christ, he cannot stand by silently while innocent people are being terrorised and having their throats cut. No ideology, he states, can justify such an approach whether it claims its authority from God or from the state. His editorial ends: 'God's glory is revealed in the face of a child. Up until her death Odette carried this imprint which nothing can erase, for no one can quench the fire of God's love. May this fire be born again out of the ruins and cinders accumulated in Algeria.'[17]

On a less angry note in another *Le Lien* editorial in May 1996, 'Un Souffle de Liberté' ('A Breath of Freedom'), Pierre counselled his flock 'to hold on to their confidence and not to become discouraged, to maintain hope and not to give up, not to allow love to die despite the rage in one's heart, to desire peace and to painstakingly build it, not to follow the pack, to remain free in chains... isn't this a way of living from the Spirit?'[18]

A QUESTION OF PRUDENCE

In an interview on *France 2*,[19] a national TV station, on 10 May 1996, just under three months before his assassination and while the monks of Tibhirine were still being held by their kidnappers, Pierre was calm and somewhat upbeat, hopeful about the Christian presence in Algeria. He said that the Christian community intended to remain in Algeria because they didn't wish to abandon their friends in their hour of need: 'It's a matter for us of fidelity in the name of our faith but also in the name of simple human solidarity.' When asked if the Muslim population desired this solidarity, he replied: 'It's precisely because there is a response from the Algerian Muslims that we feel supported in our stance. We are being sustained at this moment as we have never been before.'

Regarding the persecution of Christians in Algeria, Pierre replied: 'I think that what is happening in Algeria at present isn't an Islamo-Christian debate or an attempt to eliminate Christians, even if unfortunately we feature in this debate. It is first of all an Islamo-Islamic debate. It is a war between differing understandings of Islam and in my opinion is very serious.' Did he feel personally threatened: 'Not really. Life continues, daily life continues and when one lives the events of everyday life one doesn't think about fear.'

The interviewer concluded with the question: 'Do you consider the risks you're taking, passing through Paris, by expressing yourself on television, *France 2*, this evening? And why this risk?' Pierre: 'I'm taking this risk because through this programme I would like to emphasise that this solidarity which we have sought, which we have desired, which we have attained over many decades, we still desire it today at a time when conflicts between cultures and religions are becoming worse, at a time when exclusion and marginalisation exist; well, we hope to send out a message of peace by our very existence.' Unfortunately, as we know, Pierre's optimism about his safety proved to be unfounded.

The French television interviewer questioned Pierre about his awareness of the risks he was taking by allowing himself to be interviewed on *France 2*, at a time when eleven of his fellow-Christians had been assassinated in Algeria and the monks of Tibhirine were being held captive. His replies to the interviewer's questions were calm and irenic in contrast to the bluntness and forthrightness of some of his editorials in *Le Lien*. Some people thought that Pierre was being imprudent and putting his life at risk by this outspokenness. Was this an example of his 'impulsive' nature or the courage of a prophet?

IS PRUDENCE ALWAYS THE BEST CHOICE?

When I put these questions to those who knew him well at the time, I received conflicting answers. First of all, was he impulsive? Mgr Claude Rault, Bishop of Laghoaut,[20] agrees that Pierre was impulsive but he saw no sign of nervousness about him. (His father had once described him in November 1968 as having an 'impulsive even nervous temperament'.[21]) He thought that his editorials reflected his impulsive nature. Mgr Rault remarks: 'Another quality which I noticed in him was a sense of justice. He couldn't tolerate abuses committed against little ones and the weak.' Pierre couldn't abide injustice or duplicity and responded forthrightly.

Mgr Teissier, Archbishop of Algiers, 1988-2008, and Pierre's predecessor as Bishop of Oran, didn't think that Pierre had an impulsive personality but rather that he couldn't tolerate prevarication, half-truths or violence: hence his straight speaking. His sister, Anne-Marie wrote that 'he could be impulsive but I do not remember that it led to erratic behaviours on his part.' And Jean-Jacques Pérennès OP commented: 'Pierre was perhaps impulsive in his youth but this was no longer true after that. He was, on the contrary, a very deliberate, very restrained person who controlled himself a lot.' Thierry Becker said that he saw no sign of a nervous or impulsive personality during Pierre's time as Bishop of Oran.

As regards being imprudent, Mgr Tcissier wrote that he had often 'advised him to be more reserved in his press statements but he promptly replied that he didn't wish to be a dumb apostle whom one could accuse of remaining silent when it was necessary to speak out.' Mgr Teissier went on to say that Pierre was freer to speak out than he because Oran was farther away from the centre of power and, in addition, no members of his flock had been assassinated.[22] 'Personally I didn't wish to be put in a situation where I could be held responsible for an assassination attempt upon us as a result of injudicious comments made by me.'

Mgr Rault remarked: 'When I became aware of this editorial [Bravo!] I said to one of my friends: "Pierre will be the next." ... I don't know if he lacked prudence. I believe that it was a prophetic audacity, similar to that of Jesus before the Pharisees ... He must have known that this denunciation would lead to his condemnation; he wasn't naïve ... His desire for truth led him to his own assassination.'

Anne-Marie wrote: 'Impulsive, it's possible, wounded to his very core certainly, and as he had a means of expressing himself publicly he made use of it. A lack of prudence ... is prudence always the best choice? I don't know.'[23] As for Jean-Jacques Pérennès OP: 'I was among those who reproached him for his "imprudence". In fact, it was courage. And not at all impulsive because as I've said above, he was a person who controlled himself a lot, almost too much.'

Thierry Becker, his Vicar General, has the last word to say on this question: 'The editorial in *Le Lien* "Bravo" after the assassination of Sr Odette was an outburst of anger, in my view perfectly justified, which was in no way provocative and helped to open people's eyes. It was well received in the diocese.'

The editorial, 'Bravo!', reminds me of the Old Testament prophets who spoke out fearlessly against injustice and profiteering and of Jesus' condemnation in St Matthew's Gospel of the hypocrisy of the Pharisees. And, inevitably, Pierre would suffer the fate reserved for them. Pierre had the 'fire of God's love' burning brightly within him and couldn't remain silent in the face of injustice. He was a person who spoke the truth in love, who abhorred hypocrisy and double-dealing. Pierre wrote in an editorial in *Le Lien* in March 1996, just five months before his assassination: 'He [Jesus] preferred to follow to the end the logic of his life and of his mission rather than to betray who he was, what he said and what he did, by abandoning or denying it in order to avoid the ultimate confrontation.'[24] Pierre was following in the footsteps of Jesus who had refused to remain silent in the face of the religious hypocrisy of his day. Like Jesus, Pierre too paid the ultimate price for refusing to compromise with the powers of darkness.

Part 2

The Presence of Someone

The Eucharistic gift of self was at the heart of Pierre's spirituality

9

A Spirituality of Encounter

HOW CAN the Christian Church justify its presence in an overwhelmingly Muslim country like Algeria? Many Muslims, will, understandably, see the Church's sole aim as being to convert them to Christianity. And that would have been true for the vast majority of missionaries in the nineteenth century.

Today, perhaps the simplest and most convincing justification for a Christian presence is that given by Fr Marius Garau who spent many years sharing the life of the Tunisian people. In his book *La Rose de l'Imam*[1] he recounts the deep friendship which he developed with Si Ali, the Imam of the Great Mosque of Gafsa. Si Ali developed a severe flu and Marius, as his friend and a qualified nurse, looked after him during his illness. Si Ali thanked him warmly for his ministrations and added: 'I know why you, and the sisters, have come to Gafsa; you wish to show the love of God by living according to the Gospel.'[2] Si Ali had put his finger on the reason for the Church's presence in overwhelmingly Muslim countries. Her primary purpose is to share with her Muslim brothers and sisters something of the life and love of Jesus Christ.

At his installation as Bishop in Oran on 9 October 1981 Mgr Claverie put forward a similar justification for the Christian presence. First of all, he stated clearly what being a missionary Church didn't imply: the Church wasn't an aggressor, an agent of neo-colonialism, nor did she engage in proselytism. He then went on to describe positively the Church's mission, echoing quite strongly the words of Jesus at the start of his public ministry in the synagogue at Nazareth:[3]

> But we are and we wish to be missionaries of the love of God such as we have discovered it in Jesus Christ. This love shows an infinite respect for people and doesn't impose itself, imposes nothing, doesn't violate consciences or hearts. Delicately, and by its very presence, it frees that which has been chained up, reconciles that which has been violently separated, puts on its feet that which has been crushed, restores to a new life that which was without hope and without strength. We have known and believed in this love: we have seen it at work in the life of Jesus and in those who live by his Spirit. It has seized us and swept us along. We believe that it can renew the life of humanity if only we will acknowledge it.[4]

The Algerian Church expresses the same idea when it describes itself as being a Church of Encounter and the expression 'the sacrament of encounter' (*le sacrement de la rencontre*) has been coined to express this reality. Christoph Theobald SJ has written an insightful book, *Gospel Presences: Reading the Gospels and the Apocalypse in Algeria and elsewhere*,[5] the fruit of his seven visits to the Algerian Church, in which he tried to help the tiny Christian remnant articulate a theology of presence in an overwhelmingly Muslim country. His theological explorations focused on a close reading of the Gospels and the Book of Revelation where he sought to discover how Jesus, and his first followers, interacted with the surrounding culture and proclaimed the Good News of God's love and forgiveness. His theological reflections could best be described as a sacramental theology, discovering God's presence in the everyday lives and events of everyday people, a God who was, and who is, active through the Holy Spirit both inside and outside the institutional boundaries of the Church, a God who is present and active in all people of goodwill.

A sacramental approach to life is particularly relevant in a Muslim country like Algeria where the small Christian community cannot openly evangelise for fear of being accused of proselytism. Their message must be conveyed more by signs or actions than by words. Pope John Paul II referred to this during the 1986 *ad limina* visit of the North African bishops. He remarked over a meal that 'basically you are living what the Council says of the Church. She is a sacrament, that is to say a sign, and one doesn't ask of a sign that it be many.'[6]

SACRAMENTS MAKE CHRIST PRESENT

In the era preceding the Second Vatican Council the notion of sacrament tended to be used exclusively for the seven sacraments which, it was taught, could be directly related to the life of Christ as portrayed in the New Testament. Since the Council the idea of sacrament and sacramentality have begun to be understood more broadly. The primary sacrament or sign of God's presence in the world is Jesus who revealed to us in human form the face of the transcendent God. And the Church, in its turn, is Jesus' visible presence in the world, a sacrament, or sign, of his presence. As the Second Vatican Council puts it: 'the church, in Christ, is a sacrament – a sign and instrument, that is, of communion with God and of the unity of the entire human race.'[7] John Macquarrie sums up current understanding as follows:

> Christ we must recognize as a super sacrament, a unique manifestation in visible form of the authentic life of God. The church, too, as the dispenser of sacraments, is of a different order from the sacraments which it dispenses.... Christ is the sacrament of God; the church is the sacrament (body) of Christ; the seven sacraments are the sacraments of the church; the natural sacraments scattered around the world are, from

a Christian point of view, approximations or pointers which find fulfilment in the sacraments of the gospel.[8]

All of the Church's sacraments find their source in the life, death and resurrection of Christ and it is the Church's privilege and responsibility to be the channel of his life for others. Jesus is the source and the minister and the content of all of the seven sacraments. Hence when a person baptizes he acts in the place of Christ and it is through Christ's power, his Holy Spirit, that the new life of Christ is bestowed upon the person being baptized. The sacraments are always about a relationship with Christ, about growing into the fullness of his life. So not only is every human being made in the image and likeness of God but through the sacraments of the Church this image and likeness, damaged by sin, is constantly being renewed and restored.

The universality of God's offer of salvation in Jesus Christ was strikingly highlighted in *Gaudium et Spes* when the Council Fathers taught: 'For by his incarnation, he, the Son of God has in a certain way united himself with every individual.'[9] This teaching was re-iterated by Pope John Paul II in *Redemptor Hominis*. Thus through the incarnation every person, by the very fact of their humanity, enters into a relationship with God through Jesus Christ. The Holy Spirit continues to work through the Church but the Spirit is also active in the hearts of those outside the visible Church who work for the betterment of the human family. John Macquarrie writes: 'Perhaps the goal of all sacramentality and sacramental theology is to make the things of this world so transparent that in them and through them we know God's presence and activity in our very midst, and so experience his grace.'[10]

SACRAMENTS ARE ABOUT RELATIONSHIPS

Sacraments, at their heart, are about relationship, relationship with Christ, relationship with other people and relationship with ourselves. So Baptism, as well as giving us God's life, also incorporates us into the fellowship of the Church, and establishes us in a relationship with the members of the Church in our local community. As baptized members of the Church we are members of Christ's Body. And as such we are called to become visible signs of God's presence and love for everyone we meet, sacraments of God's loving presence for those both inside and outside the Church. This looser use of the word 'sacrament' reminds us that we are all called to be 'ambassadors for Christ', [11] to bring his love and his presence into the life of the world, through our relationships, our words and our actions all of which are an expression of our life in Christ: 'In our mutual relations we are there for others, a sacrament of God in Jesus Christ.' [12]

It is understandable that Pierre, living in an overwhelmingly Muslim community, should give prominence in his teaching to the sacramental presence of the Church. He writes: 'To be insignificant, as we are, a tolerated minority, has led us to stake the main part of our mission on the quality of our encounters.' [13] Writing in *Le Lien* in 1987 Pierre remarked that with the ongoing 'Algerianisation' of the country, *i.e.*, the increased use of Arabic and the growing emphasis on the role of Islam, the tiny Christian minority could feel marginalised and tempted to withdraw into its own closed space of liturgical life and Church gatherings. However, the very greatness of the Christian way of life comes from its love of God and love of neighbour which is expressed in relationships. So regardless of their numerical size or influence, their life and mission depend on this witness: 'It's not an exaggeration to say that, for the Christian, relationship is an absolute: God, in his intimate being – Trinitarian and one – is relationship and communion. He is Love.' [14]

In a 1977 talk, entitled 'Christ and the Church, Sacraments of God's Presence in the World',[15] to a gathering of priests in Oran, Pierre addressed the question of how we can embody Christ's presence in today's world. Jesus, explained Pierre, is a sacrament of God, his expression or Word, who was and who continues to be active in the world. He is the one who gives us access to the life of the Father, the source of all life. Jesus didn't come to found a new religion, one among many: 'He came to put humankind in the presence of God and to reveal that God is the very source of all life because he is Love.' [16] And he does that for all people through his life, death and resurrection. To gain access to God, says Pierre, we have to follow the same route that Jesus followed: 'All the living will only live if they consent to die to themselves, completely abandoning their pretensions and self-importance in order to gain access to "justice", to a right relationship with the Source of their Life. And that applies regardless of a person's religion or ideology.' [17]

If we live according to the Spirit then the living and active God dwells within us and we become a sacrament, a sign of God's love, for others: 'Our *raison d'être*, our vocation, our mission are therefore dependent on our manner of being present to the Presence.' [18] The Church's mission consists in gathering together all those who wish to follow Jesus' path, a path which gives access to communion with the Father. In becoming Jesus' presence, the Church becomes a source of life for everyone: 'The Church is "missionary" by this particular mission and for every person – otherwise she is only one new religious club among many.' [19]

MAKING PEOPLE WHOLE AGAIN

In the encounter between Christian and Christian or Christian and Muslim, the sacramentality is first and foremost relational. Fr Christoph Theobald writes: 'Spontaneously we identify sacraments with *religious rites*; now in the Christian tradition, it is first of all persons (and I add) in relationship who are sacraments: Christ *for* those whose path he crosses, the baptized person on the Galilean roads of today, the husband for his wife and the wife for her husband, the ordained minister for their community, etc.; all of those are "sacrament-people", as Congar puts it, insofar as, *by their simple presence,* they are in a *significant relationship with others.*' [20]

Pierre expresses the same idea when he writes: 'I believe that Jesus' greatest miracle was to recognise people who lacked recognition: prostitutes, sinners, publicans, even possibly Pharisees, people who were despised, excluded, who found again their existence in his presence. And, he didn't ask them to follow him; he converted them simply by looking at them, or rather he gave them back their human dignity; and following on from that he gave them the possibility of living.' [21]

The sacrament or the outward sign lies in the relationship established with another person, a relationship which becomes a source of new life for both parties, similar to the relationship of the Good Samaritan with the man who had been mugged and left by the roadside. In sacramental relationships it is not so much the help given which is primary as the quality of the relationship established. It is the relationship which heals the other. 'All the Fathers of the Church have told us in their own way: *wherever there is a real relationship, there is the Word.*' [22]

This core insight explains so much of Pierre's daily living out of his baptismal and priestly ministry. Given the gradual disappearance of the Church's institutional structures after independence in 1962 and the final *coup de grâce* in 1976 when the socialist government nationalized the Church's remaining schools and hospitals, the Algerian Church could no longer rely primarily for its witness on its institutional structures. The Church does still run student libraries, women's support groups, etc., but on a much smaller scale and its witness now largely depends on the quality of its face to face encounters with individuals, a quality of personal presence.

Pope Benedict XVI, in his first encyclical, *Deus Caritas Est*, describes what this encounter calls for: 'Seeing with the eyes of Christ, I can give to others much more than their outward necessities; I can give them the look of love which they crave.' [23] This is a much more demanding kind of witness as it pre-supposes an inner transformation on the part of the person witnessing: Christ's love has to be visible in their words and above all in their actions. The person can no longer hide behind the institutional face of the Church. This helps us to understand why Pierre stressed so much in his preaching and writing the importance of a life of prayer, community and service. Otherwise, Christ's transforming love will not take root in us. And without this personal and communal transformation, the Church becomes, at best, just another enlightened NGO.

TO CONQUER DEATH HERE AND NOW

What is the ultimate source, the wellspring, of these sacrificial relationships which show forth Christ to the world? For Pierre, Jesus' relationship with the Father as portrayed in St John's Gospel gives us the answer. The most important title of Jesus, writes Pierre, is that of Son of God. Jesus reveals his full identity in his relationship with the Father as Son; it is from the Father that he receives his being and his mission: 'He directs us towards the Father and gives his life to reconcile us with Him, in a filial communion: it's the very purpose of his mission. The Good News has no other content: to reveal that God is Father, and to allow us to live as sons [and daughters].' [24] Sacramental relationships depend on our being united with Christ, on our having his Holy Spirit dwelling within us. Without the presence of the Holy Spirit we cannot be Christ for others, for those whom we meet in our daily encounters. The ultimate source of our life-giving relationships is the Spirit who lives in us, establishing us, through our adoption as sons and daughters of God, in a filial relationship with the Father.

Jesus' filial relationship with the Father is one of complete surrender and love. As Christians we are conformed to Christ and therefore being joined to him we enter into his relationship with the Father and like him 'we become pure relationship': 'completely turned towards the Father from whom we receive life, completely turned towards people to whom we communicate life.'[25] As Pierre so often says: 'The meaning of existence (human and Christian) is to enter into the totality which is the love of God – and to welcome life as totally relational: I only exist in giving myself away, in abandoning myself.'[26] And the source of this new life is to be found in the resurrection of Jesus and the sending of his Holy Spirit.

Faith, for Pierre, grows out a lived experience and nourishes a lived relationship. Writing to his parents on April 7th, 1980, just after Easter, he stresses the importance of a faith which is a way of life and not just a theoretical construct: 'This year once again we have celebrated the victory of a certain quality of life over the realm of death, that at least is the primary meaning which I find in the resurrection of Jesus and which sums up for me the core of his message. To live from his spirit, to strive to create lovingly and to wager one's life upon this – whatever may be the other powers which control the world and the human heart, – it is here and now to conquer death.'[27]

As the Fathers of the Church say: 'wherever there is a real relationship, there is the Word.'[28] And it is this 'real relationship' which Pierre worked tirelessly to establish with everyone whom he met – whether they be Christian, Muslim or of no faith – and it was this being present to others, being Jesus Christ's sacramental presence to them and for them, which made his witness so fruitful.

10

Do Not Be Afraid, I Love You

THE KEY theme and the key word in Bishop Pierre's understanding of revelation is 'presence', the presence of a living person with whom we can have a relationship of love, here and now – today. This emphasis on meeting the risen Christ in Scripture and in other people, on becoming aware of his continuous, living presence in our lives, helps us to understand Pierre's own spirituality and that of the Algerian Church which, as we see throughout this book, is first and foremost a spirituality of encounter.

One of the advantages for Christians who live in a Muslim country is that it helps them to become more aware of their own faith, to clarify what is at the core of their own beliefs and also to benefit from the insights and example of fellow-believers in God. Pierre was the main author of *Le Livre de la Foi*[1] (*The Book of the Faith*) published in 1996 by the North African Bishops. It was designed to help Christians living in a Muslim environment deepen their understanding of the Catholic faith. It's fascinating, says Pierre, to live among a people with a different religion. Although Jews, Christians and Muslims have many common sources they all put their own imprint on them and express them in a specific manner.

In reflecting on the Christian and Muslim understanding of God, Pierre became aware of a crucial difference of emphasis. Almost every encounter with God in Christian revelation begins with the words: 'Do not be afraid, I love you'. The whole of the Good News is to be found in those few words which cast out fear. According to Pierre this is the creative word which is revealed in all the theophanies. Thus, for example, the Lord says to Moses at Mount Sinai: 'The Lord, the LORD, a God merciful and gracious, slow to anger and abounding in steadfast love...' (Exodus 34:6). And these words of love allow the prophets and Our Lady to transgress boundaries, to be creative and fruitful, to come out of their 'bubbles', and leave behind their closed worlds.

CREATES A VERY DIFFERENT TYPE OF PERSON

In the Muslim world revelation is conceived very differently; the first word is: 'Adore me, I am the One and Only'. This doesn't put the emphasis on a mutual relationship of love but focuses on the believer's duty to worship the one God: 'Therefore do not adore idols. It refers back to God. It is a very different movement [from the Christian one] which creates a very different type of person.'[2]

This is the original and only message of all the Muslim prophets, notes Pierre. As humankind degenerates into idol worship, each prophet in his turn repeats the message of worshipping the one and only God: 'Thus the prophets succeed one another without there being, at least in the Book, a spiritual experience starting from a particular life.'[3] For the Muslim there is no progression in history but a return to the original source:

Truth is to be found by going backwards. It has been given, once and for all, at the moment of creation. And since then everything can only continuously deteriorate. To restore the situation it is necessary to go back to the origins. History is a cycle in which one regains the purity of faith by always going backwards, to the origins, to creation. There is no development in history. There is an ideal type: the book, the person of the book and an ideal society defined in the book which one must seek to reproduce in history. Things have been defined once and for all and it is a matter of applying them.[4]

Pierre points out that the different understanding of revelation in the two faiths gives rise to a different approach to theology. If faith is, first of all, life, theology should be, first of all, a theology of the believing life. For the Christian, theology is concerned about the real life experience of the believer, finding traces of God alive within human experience and seeking to articulate and live from this understanding.

Muslim theology, on the other hand, stresses the unknowability of God, his transcendence, and human submission to him: 'Indeed, Islam does not consider itself to be one religion among others but truly *the* original religion, springing from a pact between the Creator and mankind and which gives to the creature his stature and meaning. Man is only man through his submission to the Creator: we are born Muslims (Islam=submission). As this submission is not self-evident and involves specific behaviour which enacts it, God constantly raises up prophets amongst men whose mission is to remind them of the original pact: "God is One, adore him" and his demands.'[5] And the *Qur'an* is the final revelation to the Prophet Mohammed which contains the fullness of this original revelation. The God revealed by the *Qur'an* is transcendent and one, who remains unknowable and can only be known through his self-revelation. In Christianity, on the other hand, notes Pierre, we have, in Jesus, a window into God, and our relationship with him is filial and not just one of submission.

AN INCARNATE OR A TRANSCENDENT GOD?

The Christian understanding of revelation is marked indelibly, says Pierre, by belief in the incarnation, God taking on human form. Thus revelation takes place as a part of human history. The fullness of Christian revelation is not found in a book, the Bible, but rather in the historical person of Jesus Christ. And Christian revelation continues to unfold, to be more fully understood in time through the Spirit-filled lives of the followers of Jesus.

Pierre remarks that Jesus wrote only on sand so that revelation would not be fossilised: 'The revelation of the divine presence comes about in and through a person, in and through the relationship with this person.... It's the impact of this presence both on people and on communities which the Epistles and the Gospels convey: they share their experience of encountering the Messiah and of what this gave rise to in their lives. Their aim is to give one access to the experience of encountering the risen Christ alive today and always, and not to direct us towards a Law decreed by the Prophet Jesus in the past. That's why the knowledge of God is never complete and the ways of encounter remain open forever.'[6] Unlike the *Qur'an* which is purely the Word of God without any human input or influence, the Bible carries the mark of the human being because it results from an encounter between humans and God. The Bible invites human beings to encounter the living God, to enter into a saving dialogue with him.

Revelation in the *Qur'an*, on the other hand, is seen as complete and unaffected by historical development. The revelation made to Mohammed, according to Islamic teaching, is the same as that made to Abraham, Moses and Jesus. However, it is free in its purity from the corruption and/or falsification to which it has been subjected by Jewish and Christian writers. For Muslims, history only provides the setting in which God reveals his divine will. In itself it has no part to play in the content or unfolding of revelation. In Islam, Mohammed merely records the words which are dictated to him by the archangel Gabriel. Humans have nothing to add to, or subtract from, the word of God which is eternal and divine in origin, not subject to the vicissitudes of time.

The concept of God taking on a human nature and participating in human history is unimaginable and blasphemous: 'They say, "The Most Merciful has taken a son." Certainly you have put forth something abhorrent! The heavens are nearly torn apart because of it, and the earth split open, and the mountains collapse in pieces – that they should attribute to the Merciful a son, when it is not fitting for the Merciful to take a son' (*Qur'an* 19:88-92).[7]

THE SHOCK OF AN ENCOUNTER

Pierre writes that the books of the Bible 'in their final state, that in which we know them, are indissolubly a human and divine work. On account of this, the Christian idea of revelation differs profoundly from the Muslims one.'[8] By contrasting the Christian and Muslim understanding of revelation, Pierre is able to better highlight what is specific to the Christian understanding of Scripture, namely that Christian revelation is above all personal, centred on God's presence in human history and his self-disclosure in the person of Jesus.

A key statement from the Second Vatican Council text *Dei Verbum* succinctly states: 'The most intimate truth thus revealed about God and human salvation, shines forth for us in Christ, who is himself both the mediator and sum total of revelation.'[9] And this personal self-disclosure does not end with the death of Jesus but is available to each believer in God's living Word which continues to encounter us in the now of today: 'To surrender oneself to the Word of God isn't a matter of admiring it, dissecting it, or repeating it by heart, nor of obeying it as one obeys commandments, but of entering into a living relationship with the one who utters it.'[10] This understanding of revelation as primarily personal and secondarily propositional can be seen in the priority which personal encounter had in Pierre's pastoral outreach, his friendships and in his prayer life.

'Jesus for me is someone who awakens and initiates one into the Presence.'[11] The biblical writers, notes Pierre, are, above all, trying to express 'the shock of an encounter with Someone whose Name is still unknown and whose presence they are going to laboriously discover in the events of the course of history.'[12] Not only do the inspired writers wish to share their own personal encounter with the living God but they also wish to enable others to have the same experience: 'To open the Book is to put oneself in the Presence of Someone who I believe, with the sacred writer, wishes to enter my life today and to enable me to welcome his word.'[13] For the Christian the essential encounter is with the person of Jesus.

A TRANSFORMATIVE PRESENCE

The New Testament focuses on the impact which Jesus had on his disciples and opens up the possibility for each of us to share in that experience: 'The core of the message to which I adhere is to be found moreover in this affirmation with which the Christian faith distinguishes itself from the Jewish faith and developed its distinctiveness: it is possible to encounter Christ today because he has been raised from the dead and is alive.'[14] This encounter, however, will not be painless or self-evident. It demands, writes Pierre, like the Exodus experience of the Jewish people, a going out from self, a leaving of self behind, a passing over from death to life.

The writers of the New Testament recount what Jesus said and did. What is more important is their transmission of the impact he made upon them by who he was, his personal encounter with them. It was their encounter with his person, both words and presence, which was transformative: 'His presence then becomes for them an effective sign of divine action and it makes a powerful and deep impression on the disciples: it impresses itself as it were on them, it inhabits them, and it is to this influence that we owe the Scriptures.'[15]

In reading the Scriptures, Pierre states, we are not primarily looking for teaching, information, miracles or pious stories. Like the first disciples we are looking to meet a living person, to have a living relationship: 'God becomes flesh in historical time to open me up to the presence and action of God. The Gospel is not first of all a book but an event; the coming of Jesus.'[16] The Scriptures open up for their readers the same possibility of encountering the Risen Jesus as was the case for those men and women whose lives were transformed so long ago by encountering him in Galilee. The Christian community, the Scriptures and a personal experience of Christ are the framework then and now of revelation: 'These three elements constitute the framework where Revelation is brought about and what unifies them is the presence of Christ.'[17]

A MEETING WITH THE RISEN CHRIST

What gives a unity to each of the Gospels, says Pierre, made up as they are of so many different elements: 'events, characters, reflections, interpretations, exhortations, teachings ... is faith in the risen Jesus.'[18] The Holy Spirit, who inspired the biblical text, speaks to the Spirit in the hearts and minds of readers to give them 'access to the mystery of Christ.'[19] In this reading of Scripture, through the eyes of faith, the religious and moral teaching, parables and miracles all come together to enable us to meet the person who is at their origin and 'who beckons us to follow him.'[20]

Jesus' resurrection cannot be reduced to a current affairs item, a fact of history, but requires an act of faith: 'The risen Jesus establishes with each one to whom he makes himself known a relationship in which he has the initiative.'[21] He makes himself known through signs: Mary Magdalene is called by name; on the road to Emmaus he breaks bread; at other times our minds are opened to recognising him through the reading of Scripture: 'Among the many signs which he addresses to me the Gospels constitute the reference and the principle of interpretation which allows me to decipher them and make sense of them.'[22] In reading Scripture, cautions Pierre, we mustn't objectify the text by focusing on historical facts. The *ipsissima verba* of Jesus or past events are not what is important. Rather it is a question of making contact with 'a presence who invites me into a relationship without which I can understand nothing'.[23]

That's the reason why, for Christians, the core of revelation is not a book but the person of Jesus. The quality of his presence, of his being, radiated the presence of God more powerfully than any words ever could. As followers of Jesus the most important thing is to 'search for God's presence and to adjust our life to this presence of God.'[24] When we meet with God in our lives, says Pierre, he summons us out of ourselves and gives us the strength and confidence we need 'to enter into life, the key to which is relationship with others.'[25] This 'radical confidence' in God's active presence in our lives enables us to face up to the challenges of life. In Scripture God enters into a dialogue with us, he shares his presence, his very being with us.

INTIMACY AND FREEDOM

In Pierre's understanding of Christian revelation we can see a stark contrast with the Muslim approach: 'The originality of Christianity is to make people creators, to open up the doors of the future for them where Christ goes before them and calls them. The originality of Islam is to re-assure people by giving them the key to their salvation in a Book. That is why serenity (sometimes fatalistic) is innate to them.'[26] Thus, two different conceptions of salvation history are at work: 'Man can therefore be considered either as an unchanging being, conceived from the beginning in the perfection of his nature and who must seek to return to this prototype – or as a being in becoming, a vocation which is fulfilled in history subject to the risks of freedom and contingency.'[27]

Pierre highlights the intimacy and freedom which the incarnation and resurrection of Jesus open up for Christians in their relationship with the triune God in contrast to the Muslim emphasis on God's transcendence. However, as Pierre notes, these distinctions aren't as clear-cut as a theoretical understanding might suggest. De-

spite the Muslim emphasis on the otherness of God and the honour
we must pay him 'there is also in Islam, a very strong awareness, and
especially in the mystics and in popular religion, of the closeness of
God.' [28] Very many women who have no theological education live a
very intimate relationship with God, says Pierre, and their prayer is
not limited to ritual prayer as is the case for many of the men.

The nature of revelation, how we come to know and encounter
the living God, is a recurrent theme in Pierre's spiritual writing. The
realisation that Christian revelation is ongoing and personal, and
not primarily propositional, that the person of Jesus Christ is 'both
the mediator and the sum total of Revelation' [29] is the key to Pierre's
spirituality, a spirituality of presence and encounter.

11

There Is Someone in His Life

PIERRE tells the story of a Muslim convert whose journey to faith appeared to be faltering. For several years he had attended a Christian discussion group and enjoyed the experience. His participation showed a great appreciation and understanding of the Gospels. He appeared to be a natural Christian ripe for Baptism, and yet he was unable to take that step. Although he understood very well Christian teaching, he understood it from the outside. Then one day he became a Christian. What happened? ' "I became a Christian because one evening, suddenly I realised that there were seven of us physically present but in reality we weren't seven but eight and that there was Someone there who said nothing, perhaps did nothing, but whose presence changed everything". That is faith.' [1] Pierre comments that one can read the Gospel for years on end, one can 'live' for years and then one day one discovers Someone and that changes everything: 'The leap of faith is to live in the presence of Someone and subsequently to search for this presence in every event and in every person.' [2]

Being present, notes Pierre, has nothing to do with being physically present. We can describe an object from the outside: it is there but we don't say that it is present to us. We don't establish contact with a living person by merely describing their physical attributes or having them physically present. One of the striking things about the Gospels, says Pierre, is that we have no physical description of

Jesus, his hair or eyes or anything like that. He is never described as if he were a mere object but he is experienced through signs: he makes himself present to his disciples by his look, by his word. One makes oneself present through signs, not by just being physically discernible: 'We can only discern the presence of someone when we enter into a relationship with them. Whoever says presence says relationship and this relationship is begun, is established through the signs which we make to each other, and the sacraments are the signs which Jesus gives us. The risen Jesus is not present after his resurrection in a different way from before, it is exactly the same kind of presence.'[3]

THE POWER OF A LOVING PRESENCE

When Jesus was with his own people in Nazareth, observes Pierre, they failed to recognise him for who he was. They couldn't see his potential. They were blinded by what they had known about him and his family in the past. Only those who entered into a relationship with him perceived his presence, began to know him as a person. When a relationship of trust and confidence is established between two people they become present to each other. This is to look with the eyes of faith or trust. And because the people of Nazareth had no confidence in Jesus he was unable to perform many miracles in that town.[4]

It is likewise for each one of us, remarks Pierre. If we are to realise our potential someone has got to believe in us: 'In order for someone to give birth to what they are carrying in the deepest part of themselves, a climate of trust is necessary which will enable them to know themselves and to allow others to know them.'[5] In our relations with others, says Pierre, we often imprison them in their past; we refuse to believe that they can change or that they have changed. We prevent them from growing, from acting differently. If they merited our confidence then they wouldn't really have need of it. In his encounters with others Jesus refused all power based relationships (see Matthew 4:1-11): 'Jesus refuses these temptations to dazzle, to seduce, to impose himself by any power whatsoever.'[6] His only desire was to reveal God's glory, the power of His love. And it is this power of love which liberated those whom he met from the fear of assuming their own deepest identity.

Jesus' presence, notes Pierre, made a big impact upon those who met him. The crowds were struck by him because he preached with authority.[7] It was the depth of his presence to them, more so than his words, which lay behind his authority. By his presence Jesus created 'a climate of encounter ... of communion. This presence ... was a summons to life. In his presence people got back a taste for life.... A wellspring of confidence was to be found in him because he loved. He summoned to life because he loved others.... We speak of justice, freedom, truth, dignity forgetting that they cannot exist without there being presence, encounter, confidence, friendship, love; otherwise justice is merely the battle of one justice against another kind of justice which will end up by crushing the previous one.'[8]

All of this radiance emanating from the person of Jesus was the radiance of the Holy Spirit living within him, bringing in God's Kingdom. And each one of us, even if only in a shadowy manner, shows forth God's presence through the Holy Spirit living within us. As a result of the Word becoming flesh, from now on, says Pierre, all of human life has a divine significance. All of our little gestures and actions can reveal God's presence: 'From the day that God took on a human texture, every encounter is the place of a revelation, as, for example, the Visitation teaches us. Every person has an infinite dignity.'[9]

WHAT CHRIST'S LOOK CAN DO

Liberation from fear and the abandoning of masks and *personae* begin when we feel that we exist in someone's eyes, that we matter to

them. Pierre tells the story of St John Bosco's coachman who said
that 'for him [St John Bosco], I existed.' [10] If everyone whose path we
cross, says Pierre, could say the same thing about us, then that would
make us saints. When you look at the Gospels to see how Jesus encountered people you will find the same phenomenon. People existed in his eyes; they counted: 'His greatest miracles are those where
people who didn't exist for anybody begin to exist, simply because
he looks at them, because he calls them by their name. He calls them
and looks at them in a certain way. He communicates much more
in this way to his disciples than through all the marvellous physical
ways in which his power will express itself. What counts most is that
we share something of ourselves with each other. If you're looking
for holiness, if you have still a little courage left to search for holiness
in your life, reflect on that: for him, I existed.' [11]

In the story of the woman caught committing adultery, the on-
lookers who were hoping that Jesus would condemn the woman
were in fact passing judgement on themselves. Jesus didn't condemn the woman, comments Pierre, and neither does he condemn
us: 'Not only does Jesus not condemn me but he takes me as I am
and opens up before me a space where I can freely be myself. But he
does better still because he expects the best of me, with a gentleness
and an irresistible power, without forcing me, *without judging me.* I
will become aware of someone new coming to birth in me whom I
didn't know: my best self.' [12]

When we receive this liberating trust and forgiveness we in our
turn are ready to extend acceptance to others. Having received
God's unconditional love, through no merit of our own, we are empowered to offer this love to others. It is worth quoting Pierre at
length on this concept of confidence and trust which are central to
his pastoral teaching and life:

> It [God's trust] opens out for those who merit it the least a
> space of freedom and trust where they can grow because they

know themselves to be loved. One could almost speak of God's 'faith' in human beings: because He believes in them, the least can believe in their turn and grow. The healing of a paralytic is a good example of this. Jesus carries out the healing, in other words the readjustment of the body whose movement he frees, in answer to the trust of those who brought the sick man to him. But he begins by saying: 'Your sins are forgiven you'. He carries out first of all the interior adjustment, making use moreover of a divine prerogative. Then, and only then, does he say: 'I say to you: Get up! Take your stretcher and go home' (Lk 5:7-26). Faith and trust respond to each other in the exchange of a filial and fraternal relationship whereby the Kingdom of God comes about. Jesus is its Messiah.[13]

A FOUNDATIONAL WORD OF LOVE

What is the source of Jesus' freedom, of his ability to give life to others and to free them? Jesus' freedom, states Pierre, comes from the creative word of God, an encounter where he experiences the foundational word of love.

This is the source from which he lives and transmits life to others. Jesus has no need of protective barriers because this word of love has cast out loneliness and fear from his life: 'There is Someone in his life.'[14] Jesus at his baptism and at the Transfiguration hears the defining words, 'You are my beloved son' (See Matthew 3:17 and Matthew 17:5). 'For Jesus, the filial dependence upon his Father, from whom he receives love and confidence, is the source of Freedom – it allows him to have the courage to confront the forces of death and to give his life away. His freedom vis-à-vis his family, his group, his religion is great.'[15]

Jesus' liberty comes from his consenting to this source of love in his life, his filial relationship with his Father: 'In receiving himself from this source of love, he becomes a free man. He allows God to be

God. He no longer wishes to be God, or to be a God.'[16] Jesus, unlike us, is not taken up with the desire to be the centre of the universe or to become self-sufficient and to have no need of others. Because he knows that he is deeply loved, states Pierre, he is liberated from himself and can put himself completely at the service of others: 'That is what the Good News is: Jesus comes to reveal to us that in everyone's life there is Someone who loves them strongly enough, who sustains them with so much trust that they can live free and dependent.'[17]

What strikes Pierre about Jesus is his liberty and his humanity. God's human face is also what so many Muslim converts find attractive. He is accessible, someone to whom they can relate. Jesus, although very much rooted in the Jewish culture of his time, is not bound by it. He is not caught up in the closed world, the 'bubble' of the scribes and the Pharisees who are devoted to the minutiae of the Law. Jesus' liberty, comments Pierre, is based on the foundations of grace, 'because he carries within him the presence of Someone.'[18] Jesus is always responding to the call of Someone.

> What gives him strength is the call of Someone. He is always going out to meet this Someone. He is wholly turned towards Him and that's why we find him so wholly welcoming and available. Every event, every encounter is for him a sign of the coming of Someone, a sign of the presence, of the action of his Father. And every encounter carries within it a call from his Father to go out and establish with the other a covenant of friendship. Throughout all of his life, Jesus sees God approaching. God is there in all of those who will cross his path, this Father who loves him, calls him and sends him. I believe that this is how faith turns things around as compared with religious observance. Someone goes before us and has first loved us.[19]

A TRUST BORN OUT OF TRUST

For Pierre faith, hope and love come, first of all, from God: 'The source of my *joie de vivre* is knowing that God believes in me, God hopes in me, God loves me. Faith is from God. My faith is only the response to this original trust which I discover in Christ, in my personal story, in all these graces which God sends, which mark out my story, preceded by the trust of Someone.... Faith can only be a trust born out of trust. It is not something which can be improvised or which is determined intellectually. It is the response of trust to trust.'[20]

It is the same process for hope and love: 'To unleash the power of love, one has to have been loved. God precedes, Someone precedes us. We discover this Someone, either through revelation, or purely through an interior grace, or in our human history.'[21] In these encounters throughout our lifetime we discover, remarks Pierre, the power of trust, hope and love. We can know that they are from God if they make us more fruitful and life-giving in our relationships with others and allow us to make others more trusting, hopeful and loving. It is these kinds of encounters with God which humanise us rather than our own tense efforts to change ourselves or to change the world. And all of this is the work of the Spirit through whom we receive our identity and freedom.

All of the above presupposes a certain image of God, a God whose presence inspires confidence in oneself and in others. In the Muslim world, states Pierre, God is always the greatest. Their confession of faith always starts with, 'God is the greatest' (*Allah hu Akbar*). A Jesuit friend of Pierre's always felt tempted to reply to this Muslim cry with: 'God is the smallest'. And it's true, says Pierre, as we can see in the little child at Christmas. The Muslim image of God is based on expanding to infinity the biggest and the best of anything good we can imagine. The Christian God is other than any of our human representations or imaginings: 'He is other. To show that he is radically other, he becomes like a child.' [22]

As a result of living in a Muslim world, Christian beliefs take on, for Pierre, a new power and liberating force. The face of God revealed to us by Jesus is of a God who doesn't seek domination or power or glory: 'His only passion is to give his life away, and it is really a passion which impels Jesus to give his life away.' [23]

RESPONDING TO GOD'S CALL IN PRAYER

The place *par excellence* where we encounter God is in prayer. Pierre notes that prayer springs from our incompleteness: 'There is a profound "emptiness" inscribed within every person, which is like a summons to be more, to be better', [24] the desire within each one of us to enter into communion with someone. The person's desire for this fulfilment is a response to a call from God. God has planted within human beings a desire for encounter, to leave themselves behind. Without an awareness of this call to encounter someone, or at least the premonition of such a call, prayer is a more or less an empty ritual or a search for the self.

Being recollected, being centred, awakens us to the presence: 'A presence involves *a relationship with someone. Prayer is to put oneself in the presence of God* in response to his call of love: Where are you?' [25] Prayer is only possible through the Holy Spirit who creates in us the desire to have a relationship with God. 'Prayer is then a welcoming of the Spirit who puts us on the road to encountering God.' [26]

Christian prayer is founded on our filial relationship with God in the Holy Spirit: 'What is important for the Christian then is to free the Spirit within them, to free the life within them and not to make an effort through techniques, words. It is not techniques, it is not gestures, it is not rites which will create prayer but it is a confident surrender, a relaxing of our being.' [27] God is always present in our lives, adds Pierre, but we are not present to God. Prayer is there to help us to renew our awareness of God's presence in our lives.

Prayer demands that we leave ourselves behind so that we can establish a real relationship, a dialogue with the Other. When our prayer expresses a real relationship, then God can give us 'his Spirit, his Presence, his Strength, his Life, Himself.'[28] It is our consciousness of this loving Presence which enables us to trust ourselves enough to overcome our fear of opening our hands to others and welcoming them into our lives. 'Christian prayer, for me, is: here I am, my life is yours.'[29] In prayer Pierre tries to listen and to stop talking about himself: 'A time of prayer is, for me, a time of changing the way I look at others and at myself and a search for the truth of my being, of that of others before myself and before God. I can then receive others, and the events which have disrupted my life, calmly and serenely, as calls to conversion and not as acts of aggression to be repelled.'[30]

And we pray as part of a community, as part of the Body of Christ, not as isolated individuals. We say 'Our Father' not 'My Father'.

MEETING A REAL PERSON

In the inner silence of prayer we begin to discover a bedrock of stability where we can anchor ourselves and free ourselves from the restlessness and superficiality of a busy life. When we penetrate deeper into ourselves our prayer can really become intercessory, says Pierre, because we will then be sharing 'in depth, in solidarity, the sorrow of men and women, of our families, of our countries which is so much greater than our little daily dramas, so often futile. Prayer can be the place of the communion of saints, provided we make contact within us with the source of silence. The source of silence or what Meister Eckhart calls the depth of our being, the depth of ourselves, is the "place" where the Spirit of God intercedes for the whole of creation (Romans 8:26).'[31]

Pierre describes for us his experience of meeting a real person in prayer, someone hard to pin down, someone elusive and not easily depicted but who is nevertheless recognisably our loving Father:

One is very impoverished, and yet one senses clearly that there is Someone in our life, whom Jesus calls 'Father', his Father and our Father. This 'He is there' has struck me a lot. One has difficulty in seeing how, one has difficulty in meeting Him, in discerning his presence; but 'He is there'. He is Someone to whom one can speak, even if one can't succeed in explaining it. And it is 'really' Someone; not only a diffuse presence such as one contemplates in nature; not only a diffuse presence in others; but Someone who enters into a dialogue with humans, with us. That is the great discovery of the Christian faith. And that discovery is truly the work of the Spirit who makes us say 'Abba' (Father) to this Someone who gives us a new life as his beloved sons and daughters.[32]

12

The Birth of the New Humanity

ST PAUL'S spirituality is all about new life in the Spirit, life in the Kingdom, a life available to us through Jesus' death and resurrection. It is this life in the Spirit which underlies all of Pierre's teaching. The Christian life is one of transformation into the likeness of Jesus through the power of his indwelling Spirit. Above all Christian faith is founded on a personal encounter with the Risen One: 'There is no doubt for him [St Paul] nor for us: at the start of Christian conversion, there is *the shock of an encounter with the Risen One*. No matter where one is coming from: from a passive acceptance of the Christian tradition, from Judaism, Islam, atheism, the person of Jesus becomes the centre of life – or its horizon.'[1]

We don't come to know Jesus, says Pierre, in an abstract way from books but through other people who have spoken to us about him or through lives in which we have sensed his presence: 'For it isn't only the memory of Jesus which makes one a Christian – the keeping of his teachings, the imitation of his behavior – but really to believe that he is living in us, or that we are living in him. Sometimes people contrast John and Paul: they agree completely on this essential foundation. There is in us more than ourselves – or there is in man more than man (Jn 14: 15-23, Jn 15 [the vine]).'[2] In other words, Jesus isn't a figure from the past but a living reality in our lives, thanks to his Holy Spirit. We live our new life *in* him.

The Kingdom was the main focus of Jesus' preaching and work.

In Luke Chapter 4, echoing the messianic oracles of the prophet Isaiah, we read about his mission to the poor and captives of his time. It is the publicans, the prostitutes and the sinners who welcome Jesus' message, remarks Pierre, because they recognize their need for healing. Because Jesus offers us the Father's love, he offers us at the same time forgiveness and complete trust. The humble and the poor are the first to receive and respond to Jesus' invitation because they recognize their need for liberation. In this new life our relationships are radically transformed as we begin to live not for ourselves but for others.

Instead of the Pauline word 'justification' Pierre frequently describes the process of overcoming the effects of sin, of being transformed in Christ, as 'adjustment'. He explains that this 'adjustment', or entering into a right relationship with ourselves, with others and with God, is the work of Jesus because he is in a right relationship with the Father, a filial relationship of trusting love. We too can enjoy the same filial relationship which Jesus enjoys with his Father, a relationship which can transform us into the new man or woman:

> Adjustment to God which ends up by our calling God 'Father' in a relationship of filial trust and abandonment; adjustment to oneself in a newly found peace and a healing of the wounds of heart and body; adjustment to others who become beloved brothers and sisters because all are children of God with Jesus; adjustment to the world in a relationship concerned about the fragile equilibrium of nature and respectful of life in all its forms. [3]

Without the presence of the Spirit our relationships will be caught up in the struggle for power, dominance and the other desires of the 'flesh' which are contrary to God's Spirit.

ENTERING THE WORLD OF THE KINGDOM

In a retreat which Pierre gave on the Eucharist in 1981 he confided that 'the parable of the grain of wheat which dies is the central axis of my Christian life.'[4] This is the key Pauline and Christian teaching that it is through dying with Christ that we rise to new life, the life of the resurrection. Because Jesus held nothing back, because he offered his whole life unreservedly to the Father, he was able to overcome the power of evil, to conquer it by love: 'The passage from death to life is part of his very being, he passes constantly through this surrender which dispossess death and that is why he is completely inhabited by the power of Life – of the Spirit.'[5] Jesus' self-offering is the sacrament or sign of the Kingdom of God, a new way of living as children of God.

For Christians the entry point to life in the Kingdom is Baptism when God looks at us and calls us by our name. In Baptism God's Spirit invites us to share in the death and resurrection of his beloved Son, Jesus.[6] Baptism isn't a once and for all event, explains Pierre; it is rather a perpetual movement '*a continuous passage from death to life through love*, since it is the movement of Jesus' Passover: I was dead, I love, I resurrect, I live anew. Thus each time in my life that I lose myself a little, love, leave myself behind a little, I renew within myself the life of Jesus Christ: each time Jesus Christ will be born in me and the resurrection of Jesus will do its work in me.'[7]

This is the coming to birth of the new person of whom St Paul speaks – dying to self-sufficiency and self-importance and rising to a life centred on Christ and other people, the life of the Kingdom. This is '*a death to sin*, that is to say a death to satisfaction, to self-importance, to pretentiousness, the only sin in God's eyes. All the rest is either a consequence of this pretentiousness, of this self-importance, of this satisfaction, or mistakes by the poor people that we are.'[8]

The birth of this new person, notes Pierre, involves suffering and a passage from death to life, an entry into Jesus' death and resurrection, the offering of our lives in love. Pierre doesn't see suffering as something desired by God which we search out in a masochistic way; God doesn't demand of us that we suffer as a payment for our salvation. In Jesus God has taken our sinfulness and suffering upon Himself. Suffering is, rather, the pain which comes from loving in a fallen world: 'Suffering comes from the uprooting of the self in order to enter the new life of giving oneself away and of loving, [suffering] comes from sin and possessiveness (greed, concupiscence, avarice...). One only encounters God (or others) by burning away the dross of sin, by dying to the "old man". Suffering does not bring about this liberation: it is love which impels us to leave ourselves behind, but on account of sin it [suffering] is a prerequisite. To refuse suffering is never to know love.'[9]

The message of the Cross is counter-intuitive and folly to those who follow the accepted wisdom of this world: 'Only those who die out of love gain access to humanity: the Cross reveals this fundamental law "if the grain does not die..." which overthrows all the time-honoured beliefs out of which human beings have constructed their prisons. To come down from the Cross, would be to annul all the significance of the work and the message.'[10]

THE REALITY OF SIN IN OUR LIVES

As part of our journey to the Kingdom, as part of our programme of building the Kingdom, we have to acknowledge the reality of sin in our lives. First of all, notes Pierre, we have to admit to our need of others and to our need of God: 'What God doesn't want for humans is a perfection which turns them inwards and cuts them off from others; the perfection which he wishes for them is that of relationship which leads to communion. In other words, the perfection of love. Now love is a wound which makes one vulnerable and from which the blood of our heart can flow, the breath of our life.'[11]

Recognising that we are sinners is to become disposed to meet someone who can lead us to reconciliation and a life of communion with others. It's about making an exodus from our self-centred world, a world where we are imprisoned by our own self-sufficiency and complacency.

We are not being invited, remarks Pierre, to the perfection of the Law which can make us, like the Publican in the Gospel, proud of our virtue: 'Sin is not opposed to virtue, it's not a failure to keep the Law. Sin is the inward disposition which can even colour virtue, even the most noble and most perfect exterior: to be a sinner is to wish to make oneself the centre of the world – it is to be turned inward – it is to wish to be self-contained, by oneself before others and before God, to centre everything on oneself.'[12] This is how revelation, explains Pierre, understands sin, starting with Adam and Eve in the Garden: 'Sin is the breaking of the Covenant and its consequence is death or loneliness (which for the Jew of the Old Testament is identical).'[13] What is at stake is not perfection or moral virtue but the breaking of a relationship. By wishing to become the arbiters of good and evil, Adam and Eve set themselves up in opposition to God and lose the 'harmony and communion' of their relationship with God: 'Trust gives way to fear and innocence to guilt. The relationship is broken. ... God sets out in search of humankind which has gone astray. And this is what makes up salvation history: this passionate search of God who never despairs of humankind.'[14] In Jesus we see this compassion for sinners, this same lack of judgement 'the tenderness of God in action.... he elicits and encourages conversion by an excess of attentive presence and love.'[15]

There is a struggle between the old and the new man. However, one's wounds only become sins if 'they come from a refusal to love or to give of oneself.'[16] For St Paul, 'an act becomes sinful when it comes from self-seeking, from a closed and ambitious heart, concerned to seduce, to conquer in order to be adored.'[17] For Pierre, sin is about our relationship with God and with others. In learning how to love, how to recognise humbly our dependence upon God and

upon others, we find a way out of the self-centredness which imprisons us. Our salvation lies in genuine relationships, in communion.

COUNTING ON AN INNER POWER

We can try to please God by living lives of virtue, by striving for
perfection by our own willpower. Pierre doesn't think this is a good
way of leading our lives as self-made virtuous people are like smooth
billiard balls – no one can get a hold on them, make contact with
them. In addition, when two billiards balls meet they crash into one
another and part: 'I am convinced that Jesus didn't come to make
his disciples perfect and virtuous people.' [18]

Religious eventually discover that this life of 'perfection' cuts
them off from others and leads them to seek compensation for their
loneliness in power and possessions. Then they realise that 'Jesus
doesn't offer extra strength to progress in the way of perfection but
a new way of understanding life.... Jesus doesn't offer a perfection
acquired by the sweat of one's brow, by will power. Moreover I didn't
know very clearly what he was offering! To follow him and that's it.' [19]
And by following him one becomes detached from self-preoccupa-
tion, even pre-occupation about becoming virtuous. Gradually the
disciple discovers, a way of being, a way of life, 'not a law or a path
but the Spirit which inhabited it.' [20]

Seeking our own perfection leads to rigidity and a loss of life. We
become closed to change, like the Pharisees in the Gospel, and fail
to communicate life. It is only when we are willing to accept God's
offer of love that the power of love begins to change our lives and
the world around us: 'The day when men and women really count
on an inner power, things change. As long as they haven't counted
on it, if only a little, nothing will change. God will be exiled from
the world.' [21] Jesus wishes to shake us out of our complacency, to
breach our self-importance so that we can begin to live for others, to
give our lives for others: 'Basically, Jesus, in utter destitution, takes

us with himself as he offers his life as a gift on the cross. There is no other way if perfection is life, if life is love and if love is to give one's life away.'[22]

THE GIFT OF HOLINESS

Holiness, Pierre reminds us, is something which pertains to God alone and we become holy by receiving and participating in the holiness of God's own being: 'One becomes a saint by disposing oneself to receive the gift of God, by renouncing the effort to justify oneself, to make oneself perfect. It's a question of assuming, in Jesus' footsteps, the condition of a "servant of God", of "sons of God".'[23] Saints are ordinary people with their own failures and weaknesses. There are, comments Pierre, many areas of darkness, errors of judgement and sometimes even psychological disturbances in their lives.

Why then are they canonised? Pierre thinks that it is because there is nothing of the Nietzschean superman to be found in the Christian saint. On the contrary, their very weakness can become the source of an amazing fruitfulness when it becomes the dwelling place of the Spirit. The fruit they bear is wholly disproportionate to any effort on their part, through a tense striving, to 'change the world'. Pierre stresses that sanctity and its fruits are all about becoming docile to the work of the Spirit and about putting one's trust in God's power: 'We mustn't try to do great things, but seek rather to become a dwelling place for God's Spirit. He will do through us much more that we could do or hope to do by our own strength.'[24]

And, notes Pierre, the greatest enemy of sanctity, the thing which kills it even more than pride or vice, is mediocrity: 'Pride, vice, can open a wound in a person and bring about painful, but deep, conversions. Mediocrity drowns everything, blunts everything, and sends everyone to sleep in a boredom from which we are perishing today.'[25] Pierre exhorts us to leave this condition of mediocrity behind and to enter the fire of purification, to put half-heartedness to flight – not to open our doors, only to keep people standing on the threshold. We need to leave ourselves behind. As the great Muslim mystic, Rumi, said: 'There is only one step to take in order to reach God, a step outside oneself.'[26]

The secret of sanctity is love. All of us, remarks Pierre, even in our weak and vulnerable human nature, have a great capacity to love which can be released in us through the action of the Spirit: 'Sanctity is not reserved for statues, for heroes and for "plaster saints"; it is for everybody, everybody in their own way and that way is the gift of self without ulterior motive. God makes us participate in his holiness when we follow Jesus without ulterior motive and when we learn – with him and through him – to give our life away without counting the cost.'[27]

AN EVERYDAY SPIRITUALITY

Pierre's spirituality was down to earth and incarnational. He believed in the importance of those little everyday acts of kindness which go into building up each other in community life. Holiness is to be found in the quality of those everyday encounters: 'Take any one of our days in community or at work and let us try to do what we would like others to do to us: to *greet* the other in the corridor, to *show interest* in the other (without being intrusive), *to thank* the other for any assistance or gesture, *to smile* at whoever one meets; *to be attentive* so that no one is forgotten, left alone or abandoned in a corner; ... during the day *to ask* for help (often more charitable than giving help – encouraging the initiative of others), to *welcome*, without flinching, whoever knocks at the door. To do all of that, although it may appear simple, one will need to have made the beatitudes the rule of one's life and welcomed the Spirit of Jesus Christ.'[28]

The life of the Beatitudes, the life of the 'new man or woman', is all about living in the power of the Spirit. Pierre was a charismatic with a small 'c'. In March 1980 he met a Charismatic group who talked about their experiences of the Spirit. He was rather puzzled by their world of constant signs and wonders. He wasn't attracted to, or impressed by, their experiences: 'A strange world of very sympathetic people but who operate in a world of permanent miracles, of obvious signs, of enthusiastic effusions, of "speaking in tongues", etc., completely disconcerting.' He went on to say that many young people found comfort and inspiration in the movement. However, similar healings and prophecies can be found, he remarked, among African witchdoctors, Buddhist monks and Mexican Indians: 'It's a case of a universal heritage which has nothing religious about it and which needs to be "converted". My question to the Charismatics is not so much about whether the events they recount are true, but rather what do they do with them? What do they change in their lives?' [29]

I find Pierre's reaction and comments revealing of his own spirituality and theology. Like St Paul he is not dazzled by great deeds of heroism or outward displays of faith. The key questions are: What difference does it make to the way you live? Are you becoming more loving? What counts for Pierre is the gift of love which shows itself in patience, kindness, perseverance and all the other everyday gifts which St Paul enumerates in 1 Corinthians 13 and elsewhere. In our lives what's important is not to work signs and wonders but continually to die to self, to our own selfishness and sin. The key to sanctity for Pierre, the coming to birth of the 'new man or woman', the new humanity, is love, God's love for us and our free response to this unmerited gift – a life of holiness.

Part 3

....

Understanding Islam

*The majority of churchgoers are now sub-Saharan students
with scholarships given by the Algerian government*

13

The Law, the Prophets and God

GOD EXISTS and God is someone. Muslims by the public practice of their religion recall unashamedly and collectively this fact to us, says Pierre. They also remind us that there is only one God and that the worship of anything or anybody else is idol worship. Muslim life is built around their confession of faith: 'God is the greatest. There is no god but God and Muhammad is his messenger', which the loudspeakers broadcast from the mosque five times a day. Many Westerners recover a sense of God's presence in daily life, remarks Pierre, when they're exposed to this public expression of faith in God.

Although Muslims and Christians use the same words to describe God – God is one, creator, all-powerful, merciful, for example – the word 'God' doesn't necessarily have the same meaning in the two religions. The words 'law' and 'prophet' are other instances of words common to both faiths but which are understood differently by Muslims and Christians. The concepts of God and the law have huge ramifications for the way believers view the world and live their daily lives. If both traditions are to understand each other better, the different meanings and connotations which these and other words carry need to be clarified. Pierre thinks that, by doing so, needless confusion and misunderstanding can be avoided. In addition, our appreciation of our differences and similarities will be refined, deepening our mutual knowledge, the foundation for any lasting relationship.

THE CENTRAL GUIDING ROLE OF THE LAW IN ISLAM

Law, writes Pierre, plays a crucial role in the life of the Muslim believer and is more central to their faith than in Christianity. In the original pact which God made with Adam and which is recalled by the successive prophets, God's law is revealed.

This law is found in the *Qur'an* and the *hadith* which together make up the *Sunna*, the community's way of life. The *hadith* are stories told by the first followers of the Prophet recounting either the Prophet's own commentaries on the *Qur'an* or episodes from his life. These sayings and stories haven't got the same authority as the *Qur'an* but, together with the *Qur'an*, they constitute the *Sunna*, the Muslim code of behaviour. In case of necessity the Word of God and the traditions of the Prophet can be complemented by analogical deduction (*qiyâs*) and by the infallible consensus of the community or of its jurists (*ijmâ*): 'A global vision of humankind before God and in the world, Islam scarcely experiences the need to distinguish between dogma, cult, law and morality.... It is in a single movement that the believer assents to God's existence and will: this will is presented with clarity and precision and allows them to use their reason to prolong its applications in time.'[1]

These four sources of the Muslim law allow the believer to enter on the straight way which will lead him to happiness in this world and in the next. The Muslim law, says Pierre, does not restrict itself to the religious and moral sphere of an individual's life but concerns itself also with collective behaviour and social structures. The *Shari'a* envisages that all of life, personal, political and social, will come under its rule. For the Muslim believer 'the *Shari'a* is the fundamental source of all legislation because its commandments are perfectly adapted to reason and to human potential.'[2] All of a

Muslim's life is regulated by detailed prescriptions, the best known being the five pillars,[3] leaving very little room, observes Pierre, for personal creativity.

In obeying the prescriptions of the Law 'it is a question of fulfilling together what God has prescribed for the good of the community and the authenticity of its witness. By obeying, one shows that humankind has been created by God and for God: one cannot dispose of one's life or of creation except within the limits and the norms laid down by the Creator. By submitting to the Law which express these limits and these norms, the Muslim confesses that he doesn't belong to himself but that everything comes from God and returns to God, the unique Master of the worlds (see *Qur'an* 2:156).'[4]

The Christian may wonder, remarks Pierre, if this Muslim legislation gives any room for the freedom which the Spirit brings. However, for the Muslim (as indeed for the Christian) intention is crucial in the following of the Law. Doing the right thing for the wrong reason is not sufficient. And the *Shari'a* expresses the mercy and the will of God, both of which, for the sincere believer, lead to freedom: 'Lived in the spirit of covenant, the law brings life and freedom: otherwise all law leads one deeper into sin.'[5]

THE INTERIOR DYNAMIC OF LOVE

Christianity, on the other hand, leaves more room for individual conscience and the work of the Spirit. It doesn't envisage one model of community life or one model of social belonging. Pierre writes: 'Jesus prescribes very little: he gives his Spirit. Animated by this Spirit, Christians must invent ways of behaving which best express the interior dynamic of love. There isn't a single model which would encompass all the religious and social behaviour of the Christian community. The Spirit works in very different structures without being the prisoner of any one of them and he often subverts them to make them more human, more fraternal.'[6] Jesus, comments Pierre, puts the Jewish law in its right perspective as a means to living a life pleasing to God and does not see it as an end in itself.

The law is meant to liberate and not enslave. If one follows the letter of the law then one ends up enslaved. Pierre probably has in mind in this instance the legalistic interpretation of the *Shari'a* which resembles the approach of the Pharisees to the Law of Moses, as portrayed in the Gospels.[7] Pierre writes:

> The Spirit also frees from the letter of the Law. We pass from an obedience to an exterior law to an interior impulse which orientates and gives dynamism to life. The Law with its commandments risks separating those who observe it from those who don't, the just from those who don't know it or observe it, the pagans from the sinners. It tends to imprison the believer in their complacency – righteousness is achieved by dint of effort; or in discouragement – it is beyond my reach; or in a morbid sense of guilt – I'm worth nothing in God's eyes or in anyone else's. Thus while in the beginning it was the legal code of a relationship, of a covenant, it becomes a place of separation and estrangement.[8]

The Spirit, on the other hand, restores relationships so that human behaviour finds its source and end in love: 'Thus righteousness is joined to love to realise "that which is good for humankind".' [9]

THE ROLE OF THE PROPHET

Prophets feature prominently in both Christian and Muslim scripture, the three most prominent in the *Qur'an* being Abraham, Moses and Jesus. This, however, can be a source of confusion as the Christian and Muslim understanding of the role of the prophet isn't always the same.

In Arabic there are two words for prophet, *rasûl* and *naby*, both of which are used in the *Qur'an*. The first word, *rasûl*, corresponds to our understanding of the Old Testament prophets. The *rasûl* is someone who has a specific message from God for a particular group of people in particular circumstances: 'The *rasûl* will proceed through predictions, appeals, threats, parables, mimes, poetic evocations, prophetic messages. His role is to remind people that their real history is to be found in their relationship with God – that they are beings who stand before God, for God and that that is the key to everything else, including the political, the social...'.[10] The *naby* includes all of this and more. He is, above all, the one who transmits God's eternal and unchanging message which was first revealed to Adam.

Furthermore, notes Pierre, Muslims cannot accept the weakness and sinfulness of the prophets as found in the Christian Bible and see this portrayal as evidence that the text has been corrupted or falsified. For this reason too, they cannot accept that God would have allowed Jesus to die a shameful death on the cross: 'God commits himself to ensuring their [the prophets'] final victory over all their enemies and persecutors.'[11]

Islam teaches that God made a covenant with humankind which is inscribed in human nature, in the core of our being. It is this covenant which confers on us our humanity and dignity. Adam was the first prophet who had this covenant inscribed in his heart and he lived it out more or less correctly. Since then there have been countless prophets sent by God to keep humankind faithful to the original pact with Adam, including Noah, Abraham, Moses, and Jesus. Muslims believe that all the prophets recall people to the original message which was revealed by God to Adam: 'No prophet will proclaim any other message except that of the unicity of God and of submission to His will.'[12] But succeeding generations, according to Islamic teaching, drifted away from this pact and began to worship idols. And thus God sent other prophets and finally Mohammed to recall people to the original covenant made with Adam.

That is why Muslims, says Pierre, are astonished that people continue to remain Jews or Christians because they believe that all the prophets brought the same message from God. If Jews and Christians were to discover the original prophetic book that Moses or Jesus brought, they would find that it has the same content as the *Qur'an*.

However, in the Christian tradition and in the Church today, a prophet is not the guardian of a book but someone who in the power of the Spirit witnesses to their encounter with Jesus so as to introduce us to him. In the aftermath of Pentecost 'prophecy becomes a witnessing to Jesus, dead and risen, present and active in the Church.' [13] The Muslim understanding of 'prophet' and 'prophecy', while overlapping to some extent with the Christian one, nevertheless noticeably differs from it, reflecting the different understanding of revelation in both faiths.

DO WE ADORE THE SAME GOD?

As Christians we can apply the 99 Muslim names to God. According to Pierre, in the Christian understanding of God as love all these names take on a different perspective and meaning: 'The words are the same, the content is different.' [14] The specificity of the Christian understanding of God comes as a kind of shock, remarks Pierre, when compared with the Muslim understanding. For a Christian, God's love takes us beyond the boundaries of what we might find reasonable. For Muslims, the most shocking revelation of all is the Christian doctrine of the incarnation – that God became one of us and took on human form. God is primarily known to us through the humanity of Jesus. All of our conceptions of God must be developed through our understanding of what Jesus revealed to us in his person. And that, says Pierre, gives us a different understanding of God to that of the Muslim believer.

God reveals himself to us in the words and actions of Jesus Christ. And he reveals himself to us, above all, in the scandal of the cross. For Muslims, the cross is a blasphemy as they cannot accept that God would allow one of his prophets to undergo such a shameful death. Pierre wonders if he adores the same God as the Muslim does. The contents of the *Qur'an* and the Bible overlap in many areas but the crucial difference lies in seeing things through the lens of a different interpretative key: ' "There is no God but God" is the essential Qur'anic message. God is one and, in his unfathomable mystery, he requires humankind to adore him and to follow his ways as they are defined by the books which he sent to his prophets. The same elements, in the biblical faith, are organised from the perspective of love. God is love. The whole is different.' [15] In this respect the well-known French theologian François Varillon sj made a similar point when he stated that love is not an attribute of God like, for example, wisdom, beauty or omnipotence. Rather 'the attributes of God are the attributes of love.' [16] Thus we should say that Love is wise, beautiful and all-powerful.

For Muslims, God is all-powerful and therefore can do as he chooses. For example, the virginal birth of Mary need have no other reason than God's omnipotence. The Christian understanding of God's omnipotence is different. God cannot do anything he likes because God is love and love, comments Pierre, doesn't do as it pleases. Love expresses itself in weakness because love never seeks to impose itself. Nevertheless, God's call is irresistible because love attracts everything to itself like a magnetic field and orients our freedom to its final fulfilment.

EVERYTHING IS DIFFERENT BECAUSE GOD IS LOVE

Through God's self-revelation in Jesus Christ Christians have a different understanding of who God is. To say that God is just, means for the Muslim that all our acts, good and bad, are weighed in a balance and the final judgement will be made in the light of which one outweighs the other: 'Each act is like a small pebble which is put on the scales for the end of time, each good deed and each bad deed, and at the end they will be balanced and you will be judged on the result.'[17] The Christian sense of justice as revealed to us by Jesus, says Pierre, is different. Jesus appears to sit lightly to justice. The worker who arrives at the eleventh hour receives the same wages as the one who has been there all day (Matthew 20:1-16) and the prodigal son too appears to be unjustly rewarded at the expense of his elder brother. 'Everything is different because God is love.'[18]

For the Muslim the key concept is the unicity or oneness of God: 'Each of the elements of the biblical faith [which we find in the *Qur'an*, e.g. the story of Abraham] are organised by the *Qur'an* to show the unicity of God, "There is no god but God", which is the heart of the Qur'anic message.'[19] In the Bible everything, comments Pierre, is seen and judged through the lens of a God of love who enters into a loving, personal relationship with each one of us, whereas in Islam humankind is called to adore God and to obey his ways 'as they are defined by the books which he has sent to his prophets.'[20]

Christians also believe in the one God but he is not a solitary unicity but a God of communion. Within God there is room for a relationship of love: 'Pluralism is within God.'[21] God is also a creator God but here again, Pierre points out, he is understood differently in both religions. God is not at the origin of all human acts as in Islam. There is no room in Islam for what we call secondary causes, free choices which can oppose God's will: 'The only possibility of being righteous is by entering into the will of God by totally abandoning one's own will. It is submission.'[22] Whereas the Christian God, observes Pierre, is someone who goes ahead of me, calling me, out of love, to the fullness of life. What will come to be as a result of my response remains to be decided by me: 'God and man together, in a covenant which is made today, make history.'[23] On the other hand, for the Muslim, God is someone in the past of history who has already decided everything. Thus, Muslims and Christians inhabit two highly contrasting mental worlds.

EXPLORING SPIRITUAL EXPERIENCE TOGETHER

On account of their different understanding of God, Christians and Muslims also understand prayer differently. The prominence given to public prayer five times a day in the Muslim world challenges Christians. By turning towards Mecca Muslims are once more renewing their relationship with God and proclaiming that life has no meaning except that given by the sealing of the covenant between God and humanity, represented by the Black Stone in the Kaaba at Mecca. This ambience of prayer questions Pierre but it also reminds him of the specificity of Christian prayer. In Muslim prayer 'one senses clearly, if only through the gestures alone, the believers who places themselves before a God who says to them: "Adore only me; I am the Only One". The forehead is prostrated against the ground, the gesture of a slave which denotes a great humility and a total abandonment to the Master of Judgement.' [24]

The difference between Christian and Muslim prayer, explains Pierre, lies in a different kind of relationship with God, that of a beloved son or daughter and not that of a slave. It is about encountering the living God through, with and in his Son Jesus. Christians welcome God who comes to make a covenant of love with them, who invites them into the dialogue, the communion of love between the Father, Son and Holy Spirit. With Jesus, notes Pierre, we can say 'Our Father'; we have become adopted sons and daughters. Through the gift of the Spirit, in Jesus we become 'adjusted', or put right with God and with each other; it is the Spirit living within us who allows us to exclaim 'Abba, Father' (Romans 8:15).

Despite our differing understandings of God, Muslims and Christians, says Pierre, are animated by the same Spirit: 'I don't call that in question; to live one's faith is more important than the idea which we have of God. I think that, despite their idea of God, sincere Muslims hand themselves over to God, and in handing themselves over are guided by the Spirit.' [25] God's Spirit is at work everywhere and, as far as Pierre is concerned, we will all be judged, Christian and Muslim alike, not on our words about God but on our practice of love, as described in Chapter 25 of Matthew's Gospel.

A similar point was also made in the North African Bishops' book *Le Livre de la Foi* (*The Book of the Faith*) which was edited and largely written by Pierre. In trying to encapsulate in words the mystery of God who is the Transcendent One, the bishops remind us that our words can never fully encompass him. We mustn't, therefore exclude *a priori* other approaches in the name of a spurious claim to possess the entire truth:

> Other approaches mustn't contradict what Jesus gives us to believe and to experience. Thus in our relations with Muslims we can at the same time welcome the religious process which leads them to believe in the one God, and discern in the words which they use to give an account of this faith the experiential content which they carry. In other words: what's important is to connect with the spiritual experience which both sides have, beyond the formulations, even enshrined by history, in which they express them.[26]

Thus both sides need to acknowledge the limitations of their formulations and seek to explore together the spiritual experiences which they express. Hence the vital role which common prayer and spiritual exchanges can play in promoting a greater mutual understanding and love. In his desire to be truthful in dialogue Pierre also challenges us to be honest in our use of language. By clarifying our use of theological words another obstacle to fruitful dialogue will be removed. Only the truth, as St John's Gospel tells us, will set us free.[27]

14

Christians and the *Qur'an*

I N A 1992 article, 'Readings of the *Qur'an*',[1] Pierre outlines his mature thinking on how Christians might profit from reading the
Muslim Holy Book. In the first part of this article Pierre looks at
various Muslim approaches to interpreting the *Qur'an*. He writes:
'Whatever the case may be, one must never lose sight of the fact
that the *Qur'an* is received by the Muslim believer as a divine Word
transmitted to the prophet Mohammed by the angel Gabriel. It is
free from all human alteration and presents itself as the fulfilment
of earlier revelations which it corrects and brings to their perfection
... For Muslims, the *Qur'an* is very normative on every level: dog-
matic, moral, ritual.'[2] Elsewhere, Pierre warns us that the greatest
insult one can offer to a Muslim is to suggest that Mohammed was
the author of the *Qur'an*. On the contrary, he is merely God's agent
who faithfully transmits, without addition or subtraction, what was
revealed to him by the angel Gabriel.[3]

Pierre enjoyed and valued greatly his individual friendships with
Muslims, and *vice versa*. At the same time, there is, throughout all
his writings, constant awareness of the contrast between Islam and
Christianity. Living as a member of a tiny Christian community in
a sea of Islam, Pierre honed his appreciation of the specificity of
Christian teaching and of its emphasis on the nearness of God, a
God who had pitched his tent among us. It is a little surprising then

to find an openness, on his part, to Muslim scripture as a means for Christians also to encounter God, at least to some extent. The background to this openness is a fidelity to the teaching of Vatican II on Islam, especially as found in the Declaration *Nostra Aetate*. Pierre is faithful to new conciliar developments of doctrine which highlight the role of the Holy Spirit, a Spirit of truth, who is also active outside the institutional framework of the Catholic Church. It is in the light of this teaching, and Pope John Paul II's exposition of it, that Pierre's openness to the spiritual value of the *Qur'an* can be understood. So what exactly had he to say on this delicate question?

THE *QUR'AN* IS NOT THE GOSPEL

In the past Christians engaged in a polemical dialogue with Islam where the desire was to conquer and convince rather than to understand the thinking of the other, the main points of contention being the Trinity, the incarnation, and redemption through the Cross. When the Vatican Council says, in *Nostra Aetate* (no. 3), that we esteem Muslims this was a turning point in Christian-Muslim relationships. Pierre writes:

> I cannot at the same time esteem a believer and judge the writings which he venerates as 'satanic': this is a first, important step which encourages us to read 'sympathetically' the documents of the Muslim tradition. This reading poses many questions but it also produces much wonder. There are in the Qur'an poems, cries, appeals, prayers, exhortations which express a real spiritual experience... There is also a common background with which I am familiar and where on occasion I get lost: characters, stories, allusions to biblical events, a clear and tetchy confession of the unicity of God and of His transcendence which reminds me, with its concern for justice, of the prophetic messages of the Old Testament.[4]

On the other hand, there are aspects of the *Qur'an* with which Pierre feels less at ease. He doesn't recognise the Jesus of the *Qur'an* and the Jesus of his Christian faith as being the same person. The Muslim rejection of the incarnation and of the Cross, observes Pierre, have deep roots in their understanding of God and of his relations with humankind and are not merely caricatures of Christian belief. To understand their theology more profoundly requires, on his part, that he study the Muslim scripture in greater depth. This, thinks Pierre, will enable him to discover what unites both traditions and which parts he can draw upon with gratitude. And those parts which separates the two faiths also require careful attention, if he is to discover a way of drawing closer to his Muslim neighbour 'whom Jesus asks me to love.'[5] In reading the *Qur'an*, it is important, remarks Pierre, to read it as the Muslim sacred book and not to become involved in comparing it with the Bible, which is tempting, given the many apparent similarities in characters, stories and a good part of the message. Pierre agrees with the view of A. L. de Prémare that 'the Qur'an is an interpretation of the biblical event in the light of the message and life of the Arab prophet Mohammed.'[6]

Pierre finds reading the *Qur'an* both stimulating and frustrating. Stimulating in that there are echoes of the prophetic appeals and of the transcendence of God; frustrating in that it neglects the covenant and the promise which undergird and orientate salvation history:

> Revelation is almost 'static' and is organised around a law which, through its role in human-divine relationships, and by its content, seems to me to be less advanced when compared to the revelation of the grace and salvation offered by the Passover of Jesus. ... it [the *Qur'an*] nevertheless keeps for Muslims and for us, in many aspects, *a spiritual value and certain prophetic accents*: in light of the mystical experience [of certain Sufis], one can even think that it doesn't shut the door to an intimate knowledge of a God of love.[7]

A HUMBLE RECEPTIVITY

The *Qur'an* is the spiritual heritage of an important civilisation. Pierre is impressed by the spiritual strength which many men and women find in it, a strength which enables them to cope with many problems on a personal and societal level. In the light of this lived experience of Islam, Pierre can see for himself the positive impact of the *Qur'an* on the lives of these sincere men and women. Thus those Christians who look askance at this sacred book, and see it at worst as a tissue of lies and half-truths and at best as tolerable, are blind to its positive effects. The *Qur'an* gives many humble Muslims access to a presence and to a clear message which allows them to follow a path of human and spiritual growth: 'For the Muslim the Quran is ... the sacrament of God's presence. The respect, the veneration with which this book is surrounded shows that it is not a book but the word of God. It is a presence which reveals itself and allows itself to be known.'[8]

When non-Muslims devote themselves to reading and studying the *Qur'an* they do not have direct access to this presence: 'We believe that the *Qur'an* and the Gospel only disclose their message to those who approach them bringing vital questions: for the Christian the Holy Spirit is both the one who gives birth to the question and the one who is in connivance with the text in such a way that the letter gives life. This shows the role which spiritual experience plays in understanding the message. Now we are not in a similar relationship with the *Qur'an* as is the Muslim but we can share with him the *vital question and the spiritual experience.*'[9]

The Muslim approaches the *Qur'an* in a spirit of faith; he or she believes that it contains God's living word for them. Christians approach the Bible in this spirit too. Without this spiritual belief a sacred text will not disclose its full spiritual riches to the reader. Atheists reading the Bible may admire its literary content but they won't have access to its deeper spiritual message, what Pierre calls 'a presence'. Those, however, who read the text as sacred Scripture will have access to this 'presence'. It is through openness to the Spirit that the text, inspired by the Spirit, reveals its full message to the believer.

Pierre goes on to say that if we wish, in our dialogue with Islam, to go beyond merely sharing information or polemical confrontation, we will need to share 'the vital question and spiritual experience' which we respectively bring to our religious searching. These questions and experiences are what undergird inter-religious dialogue and make it fruitful. We must, in a spirit of expectancy, seek to answer together the questions about the ultimate meaning of life, a truth which surpasses all our texts; and we must also share our search to discover the presence of God. A fruitful reading of the *Qur'an* by Christians, writes Pierre, demands that we have a living relationship with Muslim believers, whether that be through common commitments or shared prayer or spiritual emulation. Without this understanding of the way Muslims see the world, we will fail to tune into the *Qur'an*'s spiritual message: 'In this spirit [of openness] we can approach the text and work on it with a welcoming intelligence, without violating the relationship which others maintain with it and seeking in it that which God wishes to say to us through it.'[10]

In this respect the response of one of his young female Muslim friends, Oum El Kheir, after Pierre's death is illuminating. She wrote:

My friends, I'm going to let you into a secret: my father, my brother, my friend Pierre taught me how to love Islam, he taught me how to be Muslim, a friend of Algerian Christians. I learnt with Pierre that friendship is, first of all, belief in God, it is love of others, it is human solidarity. To be a Christian or Muslim came afterwards; the problem didn't arise in the Claverie School, in this school where one learnt to listen to one another, to dialogue, simply to love.[11]

THE ACTION OF THE HOLY SPIRIT

This approach presupposes that the Holy Spirit is active in the lives and prayer of other faith groups. Pierre quotes Pope John Paul II who declared at the Assisi interfaith gathering in 1986 that all authentic prayer is made under the influence of the Holy Spirit who 'is mysteriously present in the heart of every human being.'[12] He also refers to the striking statement in the Vatican II Constitution *Gaudium et Spes* (no. 22) that the Holy Spirit offers to every person, in a way known to God alone, the possibility of being associated with the paschal mystery: 'All this holds true not only for Christians but also for all people of goodwill in whose hearts grace is active invisibly. For, since Christ died for everyone, and since all are in fact called to one and the same destiny, which is divine, we must hold that the Holy Spirit offers to all the possibility of being made partners, in a way known to God, in the paschal mystery.'[13]

In the light of this conciliar teaching, Pierre goes on to say: 'it is not impossible to recognise in their words [of wise men, saints and prophets] *a certain divine revelation inspired by the Spirit*.'[14] This reasoning, notes Pierre, would also apply to the sacred books of other faith traditions, in this case the *Qur'an*:

> This recognition doesn't in any way take away from *the fullness of revelation received in Jesus Christ* and consigned to the apostolic writings. For the Incarnation does not exhaust the divine mystery and if the apostolic writings lead to an encounter with the Risen Christ, they don't imprison him within their words. They are the norm of the spiritual experience through which God continues to make himself known and communicates himself in Jesus Christ through the Holy Spirit. They do not replace him. Consequently, it ought to be possible to recognise, with Fr Dupuis, that the non-Christian holy books, including the *Qur'an* 'can be – as they have been chronologically in history – along with the Old and New Testament, diverse

ways and forms through which God speaks to humankind, through the continuous process of revelation which He makes of Himself'.[15]

Pierre notes that Fr Dupuis goes on to say that although the *Qur'an* in its entirety cannot be seen as the authentic Word of God, given that it contains error, nevertheless the divine truth which it does contain is God's Word mediated to us by the Prophet.

How can we recognise that God speaks in the sacred books of other religions? Pierre replies that if believers, through their reception of these sacred writings, produce what St Paul describes as the fruits of the Spirit, such as peace, joy, love, then we can be confident that the Holy Spirit is active through these writings. Another criterion for discerning the voice of God speaking through their scriptures, remarks Pierre, would be a willingness on the part of the readers to sacrifice themselves out of love of God and neighbour, and in this way to participate, unknowingly, in the paschal mystery of Christ's passion, death and resurrection.[16]

PRODUCING THE FRUITS OF TRUTH AND HOLINESS

Some people may consider Pierre's teaching about the *Qur'an* to be rather daring. However, it is in line with the teaching of the Second Vatican Council. The thinking of the Council concerning other faiths, and especially Islam, may eventually come to be seen as among its most important developments. Pierre, like Pope John Paul II, was committed to the insights of the Council. In *Nostra Aetate* (no. 2) we are told that 'The Catholic Church rejects nothing of what is true and holy' in other religions as they 'often reflect a ray of that truth which enlightens all men and women.' The Council discerns 'seeds of the Word' in them (*Ad Gentes*, no. 11) which the Church 'uncovers with gladness and respect' and declares herself willing to learn from 'the riches which a generous God has distributed among the nations,' (*Ad Gentes*, no. 11).[17]

The theology of 'seeds of the Word' (*semina verbi*), according to The International Theological Commission's Report,[18] goes back to the teaching of St Justin Martyr. When confronted by the many gods of the Greek world, St Justin found common ground between Christianity and Greek philosophy in their pursuit of truth through the light of reason. And as Jesus Christ, the *Logos*, is the source of all reason, 'the whole human race has participated in this *Logos*.' The participation by non-Christians in the *Logos* has been partial. Nevertheless, 'the partial and seminal presence of the *Logos* is a gift and a divine grace. The Logos is the power of these "seeds of the truth".'[19] In other words, the saving work of Jesus Christ is potentially active in the life of every human being through the presence of his Holy Spirit, producing the fruits of truth and holiness.

Pierre was fully faithful to the radical teaching of the Second Vatican Council as regards our relationship with Islam. His own experience of living side by side with devout and holy Muslims deepened his insights into the Council teaching; he was open to being enriched by the spiritual wisdom contained in the *Qur'an*.

15

Crossing the Boundaries of Difference

PIERRE wasn't afraid to say unpopular things which challenged the accepted orthodoxy of the day. This trait could be plainly seen in his refusal to paint a rosy picture of interreligious dialogue. He thought it was his duty to the truth not to paper over differences and to focus only on what both faiths held in common. He wrote: 'The most difficult thing: to meet the other and to welcome them in their difference and not in the way in which they are like me. It is there where they elude my grasp that others are themselves and can enrich me from their originality, otherwise I only meet myself and imprison myself before my own reflection.'[1]

At first sight, Christianity and Islam appear to share many beliefs and practices. While this is to some extent true, Pierre felt that this approach could be misleading. In an editorial in the diocesan magazine, *Le Lien*, in October 1986, he spoke about the chasm which separates us, a chasm largely based on ignorance, a lack of openness and fear. We can only form genuine relationships with the other, he wrote, when they are based on an honest acknowledgement of our differences as well as our similarities. This pungent editorial was an adapted version of the homily he had preached on September 28 at the priestly ordination of two Dominican friars in Lille. The first three paragraphs set the scene and are well worth quoting in full.

Plunged into the furnace, the rich man begs Abraham to send

Lazarus to him to bring him some water and Abraham replies 'Between you and us a great chasm has been fixed' (Lk 16:26). A great chasm ...

That is what we discover when we enter into a relationship with a different world: rich and poor, but also European and Maghrebi, Christian and Muslim, nationals and foreigners. Perhaps in the wonder of a first encounter we were able to believe that we could know one another and communicate. But insofar as we have not measured 'the length, the breadth, the height, the depth, the whole extent'[2] of the chasm which separates us, we haven't really encountered the other. In our relationship with Islam, for example, we haven't taken into account enough this radical difference: we thought we could find support in 'common ground' which really wasn't the case and many of our encounters were hugely disappointing.

The same goes for all of our encounters: the lack of under-standing of our differences often distorts our relationships, ei-ther because we look for what is like us in the other or because we hide our own differences believing that we will thus gain the confidence of the others. There is neither a relationship nor a dialogue because there are no longer two partners but the illusion of an impossible fusion. Recognising the existence of the chasm which separates us, whatever its nature may be, is to measure the road which has to be travelled for an eventu-al encounter. Yes, a great chasm separates us.[3]

Our first reaction to this might be discouragement and a sense of hopelessness. Pierre, however, does not wish to provoke this re-action. Rather he wishes to lay the foundations for a real and lasting relationship which will endure in good times and bad. This can only come about if we are honest about what we hold in common and honest about our differences. In a letter in 1983 to Fr Christian de Chergé, the prior of Tibhirine, Pierre wrote that the great temptation in interreligious dialogue is to focus on what we hold in common: 'On this foundation each one is reassured to find himself in the other: this is the narcissistic trap of all dialogue which tries to deny or bypass otherness. Only difference affirmed on the basis of an infinite respect for the other, in his being and his action, can motivate us to go beyond ourselves (to "transcend" ourselves) towards the Unique One.'[4]

COMMON GROUND

The Second Vatican Council Declaration *Nostra Aetate* outlines what Muslims and Christians hold in common, namely that they both worship the one God and like Abraham they try to submit to God's will for them; Muslims also 'venerate Jesus as a prophet; his virgin mother they also honour, and even, at times devoutly invoke. Further they await the day of judgement and the reward of God following the resurrection of the dead. For this reason they highly esteem an upright life and worship God, especially by way of prayer, alms-deeds and fasting' (no. 3).[5]

This ground-breaking teaching helped to overcome centuries of fear and even contempt on the part of Catholics towards Islam. A beautiful and clear exposition of the Council teaching was given by Pope John Paul II when he spoke to a huge gathering of Muslim youth in Casablanca in 1985. He outlines what Christians and Muslims hold in common and also mentions some of their differences:

I believe that we, Christians and Muslims, must recognize with joy the religious values that we have in common, and give thanks to God for them. Both of us believe in one God the only God, who is all Justice and all Mercy; we believe in the importance of prayer, of fasting, of almsgiving, of repentance and of pardon; we believe that God will be a merciful judge to us at the end of time, and we hope that after the resurrection he will be satisfied with us and we know that we will be satisfied with him.

Loyalty demands also that we should recognize and respect our differences. Obviously the most fundamental is the view that we hold on the person and work of Jesus of Nazareth. You know that, for the Christians, this Jesus causes them to enter into an intimate knowledge of the mystery of God and into a filial communion by his gifts, so that they recognize him and proclaim him Lord and Saviour.

Those are important differences, which we can accept with humility and respect, in mutual tolerance; there is a mystery there on which, I am certain, God will one day enlighten us.

Christians and Muslims, in general, we have badly understood each other, and sometimes, in the past, we have opposed and even exhausted each other in polemics and in wars.

I believe that, today, God invites us *to change our old practices*. We must respect each other, and also we must stimulate each other in good works on the path of God.[6]

RECOGNISING AND ACCEPTING DIFFERENCE

Pierre was somewhat sceptical about how much Christians and Muslims hold in common. Living in a totally Muslim environment, his perspective was inevitably more realistic than those of us who are mainly limited to book knowledge.

Pierre was appointed to the Pontifical Council for Interreligious Dialogue in 1987 and participated in three of its plenary sessions in 1990, 1992 and 1995. By temperament and conviction he believed that dialogue flourished more through personal encounter rather than in the context of large gatherings of experts and official representatives. As Jean-Jacques Pérennès OP remarks: 'All of that [various interreligious colloquiums and official publications] gave rise to many initiatives with which Pierre Claverie didn't involve himself very much because he was someone who enjoyed personal encounters and reflection rather than being a regular attender at colloquiums. He was aware of the ambiguities and risks associated with such meetings.'[7] In the dialogue with Muslims, promoted by the Pontifical Council for Interreligious Dialogue, the participants at first thought that both faiths had a lot in common, starting with belief in an all-powerful God. However, when Christians mentioned the Trinity the Muslims reacted badly. Consequently the Christian side thought, says Pierre, that it had better not mention the Trinity as it complicated things and made dialogue difficult, if not impossible.

For Pierre, this approach to dialogue is doomed to failure from the outset. We must start from our differences: 'To really have common ground we must leave behind the illusion that the words refer to the same realities. I prefer to say *a priori* that the other is other. Moreover, if he is other, it is because he is different! I take note of this difference before envisaging an encounter. I will never be the other, nor in the place of the other, however much I may desire to enter into communion with him, to know him, to love him; it's *impossible*! ... Encounter, co-existence, dialogue, friendship are only possible on the basis of difference being recognised and accepted. To love the other in their difference is the only possible way of loving. Otherwise, we tear each other apart.'[8]

And, as Pierre observes elsewhere, difference is even part of the unity of the Godhead. The Christian God is a God of communion and not of a solitary oneness: 'The core of being is communion: in God there is a place for the same and the other in a relationship of love. God is plural in his unity. Consequently the Christian world can and must accept difference whilst looking for communion. It can't be monolithic and justify this by its faith.'[9]

Pierre points out that we can react to the difference of the other in many ways – perhaps in an anxious or aggressive manner or by trying to seduce the other or win them over by generosity or kindness. However, in side-lining the other, in denying them their full existence we are at the same time mutilating ourselves: 'Alone, we are nothing. We have need of the esteem and challenge of others.'[10] And, as Pierre remarks, this need encourages us to come out of our bubbles and make contact despite our differences. This will require us to leave behind the illusion that we are the centre of the universe. The other is also looking for the truth and may have reason to see things differently from me.

In respecting the other's right to be themselves, we will need to show a certain sensitivity and wait for the opportune moment to have our say. People have the right, says Pierre, to wear masks to protect themselves and we must respect this. If we show enough trust and confidence in them the day will come when they will feel secure enough to let go of their defences.

EXORCISING A FEAR OF DIFFERENCE

In his editorial in *Le Lien* in October 1986, 'A Great Chasm Divides Us', Pierre declared that it is only when we are willing to face up to the reality of our differences that we 'are ready to recognise one another, know one another and love one another.'[11] If we are afraid of the other person because he is different, and withdraw into our own ghetto then violence and death will take over. To make any progress, says Pierre, we need to exorcise this fear of difference which renders us 'blind, deaf, dumb, incapable of communicating.'[12] Dialogue is possible only when people give each other permission to be themselves, to be equal partners.

To achieve this we need, writes Pierre, to create human spaces where people, freed from their fear, can learn to respect and love others. Pierre calls these spaces, in his own diocese of Oran, forums/ meeting places for service and encounter (*plates-formes de service et de rencontre*) where Christians and Muslims can get to know each other through shared experiences, such as libraries, centres for those with disabilities, summer camps.

In his editorial Pierre goes on to say: 'Living in the Muslim world, I know the strength of this temptation to withdraw into oneself, the difficulty of understanding each other, of mutually esteeming each other. And I appreciate fully the gulf which separates us. But before the ground-swells of violence, fanaticism, and racism which come from this, I also appreciate more the necessity and the urgency to act so that each one can leave their fears behind. To give one's life for this reconciliation, as Jesus gave his life to break down the wall of hatred which separated Jews, Greeks, pagans, slaves and free men, isn't this a good way of celebrating his sacrifice?' [13]

HISTORICAL BAGGAGE

In the November 1990 issue of *Le Lien* Pierre reflected on the historical conditioning which lies behind much of the mutual mistrust between Christians and Muslims. A common reaction in Algeria to Christian-Muslim dialogue is that when Christians were in control they tried to convert Muslims. Now that they are on the back foot, with Islam becoming stronger and extending its influence, Christians have become fearful and try to weaken Islam through dialogue: 'People say: "human rights, the secular state, democracy... these are the Trojan horses of the new Western crusade against the spread of Islam".' [14]

Behind these opinions Pierre sees an age-old humiliation imposed on Islam by an arrogant Western 'Christian' culture which saw itself as a civilising agent 'exporting its models, its goods, its missionaries ... The weight of this more recent history is strongly mortgaging every attempt to change our relationships. Still today, each side believes that it is being attacked by the other.' [15]

In Western society Pierre notes that Islam has become the new communism, the scapegoat enemy for all our ills. It is an even easier target than communism because of its more marked cultural and religious difference:

Marxism in combating capitalism operated within the same rational way of thinking. Now, by opposing Islam, one can claim to be defending one's identity, one's civilisation, one's societal vision based on the individual, reason, freedom, the secular state, democracy and human rights. The Muslim community then has the appearance of being brought together by a religion, a law, a social and confessional organisation where God's laws are the foundation and the guarantee of the human condition which is innately religious. These useful mythologies don't hold up in the face of reality but they nourish illusions and, unfortunately, also politics and the wars of 'ethnic and religious purification'.[16]

An important step, suggests Pierre, would be for Muslim and Christian authorities at the national and international level to work together in the service of values which are common to both their revelations, namely, peace, justice and the dignity of the human person. The understanding of these values by both sides needs to be discussed and clarified and promoted by official bodies in both faiths. Such practical measures, says Pierre, would give much more substances to their encounters 'which are presently bogged down in the day dreams of a powerless goodwill.'[17] Pierre acknowledges that it is more difficult for the Muslim side because the Muslim interlocutors lack the necessary authority or organisation to implement decisions taken at interreligious forums. For example, several Christian-Muslim congresses recommended that objective accounts of both sides' history should be given in school textbooks. In Europe, thanks to various episcopal conferences, catechetical textbooks have now more or less taken these recommendations on board. However, no international Islamic organisation has so far followed suit.

ADJUSTING TO PLURALISM

Another complicating factor in Christian-Muslim relations, comments Pierre, is that both sides have a different understanding of politics: 'It seems that for the Muslim, politics, is dependent on the religious domain, and should facilitate its full expression.'[18] State institutions must promote and enable the free and full practice of Islam and safeguard its values and identity. Christianity no longer demands that the state provide institutions to help it fulfil its mission: 'Negotiation then becomes difficult between groups that call for confessional political structures inspired or dictated by Revelation and others that call for *secularism* [separation of Church and State] and a political and religious *pluralism*.'[19]

Muslim countries have traditionally recognised a minority status for Christians with the right to practise their religion. Minorities are allowed to exist on Muslim terms provided they don't pose a threat: 'The Christian has indeed a place in the Islamic vision of society: respected insofar as he is a depositary of a revelation anterior to Islam; he is also suspect insofar as he persists in not recognising the fulfilment of religion in Islam; tolerated as a consequence of a bygone past which is in the process of being reabsorbed and Islamised; he is suspected of waging a permanent crusade against Islam, an eternal conspiracy which seeks to besiege and attack the Muslim fortress.'[20]

This manner of viewing minorities, remarks Pierre, will lead to a deep sense of resentment because those in the minority are not considered to be 'responsible partners'.[21] In a modern pluralist society such a position is no longer acceptable: 'It goes without saying that today in countries where secularism is more or less in place, pluralism calls not only for tolerance but respect for differences and, in any case, the political separation of Church and State. Consequently, what was once a real tolerance has become an intolerable discrimination and compromises dialogue between Christians and Muslims.'[22] Pierre wonders if the day will ever come when Christian and Muslim can make room for each other in a society respectful of each other's difference, where each is equally valued as a citizen.

As regards interaction with Muslims generally in the West, Pierre recommends that we beware of demonising Islam. The media give a lot of publicity to extremists; this in turn tends to alienate moderate Muslims from mainstream society as they feel unjustly portrayed. On the contrary, Pierre maintains that we must encourage moderate Muslims, including intellectuals, to express themselves, and help them to become more integrated, a status which many of them would like to achieve.

A LIFE-GIVING DIFFERENCE

In his 1986 homily, 'A Great Chasm Separates Us', and in the reworked version for the diocesan magazine, we can see Pierre's realisation of the magnitude of the task involved in encountering a different culture and a different religion. He realised, above all, that there was no possibility of real progress in understanding each other unless both sides 'spoke the truth in love'. Being truthful requires courage and is painful; but a failure to be so only leads to a greater estrangement and even more misunderstanding and violence.

All dialogue must have as its ultimate aim a reciprocal love. And as Fr Varillon sj points out: 'It is the distinctive feature of love to differentiate as much as it is to unite'.[23] To love another is as much about appreciating the other's difference as it is about valuing their similarity. As the doctrine of Trinity reveals, reciprocal love allows the other to be completely themselves, and by so doing achieves, paradoxically, complete union. For if the other weren't different, love would become impossible as one would be, like Narcissus, merely absorbed by one's own image. Difference is both enriching and life-giving.

Pierre, in a talk to celebrate Christian Unity Week on 19 January 1995 made a similar point: 'We [the Christian Churches in Algeria] have really ... offered the witness of a fraternal life in Algerian society, allowing it perhaps to thus discover that one can be brothers without being identical and that communion is never so rich and fruitful as when it is based on differences which are welcomed and loved.' [24]

In one of the final interviews which he gave in July-August 1996 Pierre was asked what he had gained from his contact with Islam. He replied that, firstly, he admired the Muslims' acute sense of the presence of God in their everyday lives and the steps which they took to respond to that presence. Furthermore, 'their mystics have allowed me to deepen my relationship with God through Christ, Christ as the human place where God and humanity are reconciled and adjusted, under the impetus of the Spirit of love.' [25]

In addition, he was filled with wonder by the relationship which Muslims have with their community. Muslims regard their community as a mother and are intimately affected by everything which happens to her. This sense of communion and solidarity is a stimulus for Pierre in his own Christian life: 'The Muslim way of fraternal life awakens my sense of solidarity and encourages me to re-examine my own evangelical sources.' [26]

When a person or people accept themselves and see difference as enriching, the way is open for dialogue, a dialogue which will allow both sides to be enriched and to be their best selves. And as Pierre reminds us, the opposite is also true: 'If a people or a human group chooses to isolate itself – or is isolated – by racial, cultural, political or religious segregation violence isn't far off.' [27] Pierre's analysis makes good sense of the growing tensions in Europe and elsewhere as communities, both Christian and Muslim, react in fear before difference and seek to isolate themselves from each other:

> We can never be the other or take the place of the other despite our desire to enter into a deep communion. We can only welcome each other as guests: there will be no encounter, no

communion except on the basis of an acknowledged difference; otherwise, we deny the other or we annihilate ourselves and there is no longer any encounter. [28]

16

··

Pathways to Dialogue

I N THE final years of his life, despite much suffering and many set-backs, Pierre still believed as strongly as ever in the need for dialogue and honest communication between Christians and Muslims. He saw the cross of Jesus Christ, the bridge of reconciliation, as the heart of the Christian faith. It was, therefore, the task and privilege of Christians to continue this reconciling work wherever they found themselves.

Pierre found inspiration in the teaching of Pope Paul VI's encyclical *Ecclesiam Suam*. Pope Paul describes dialogue as Christ's 'conversation' with humankind, a conversation which is at the heart of revelation and reaches its climax in prayer: 'It finds its expression in prayer; and prayer is a dialogue.' And in this dialogue with humankind Christ reveals to us 'how he [God] wishes to be known: as Love pure and simple.'[1]

In a preface for *The Sunday Missal* (*Le Missel des Dimanches*) Pierre wrote in 1994: 'The key word then of my faith today is dialogue. Not for tactical or opportunistic reasons but because dialogue is constitutive of the relationship between God and humanity and between humans themselves. I learn with Jesus that even God, to make himself known and to express his will, borrowed from humanity its words and even its flesh. I note that all of salvation history takes place under the sign of a broken and restored communication, in a dialogue where God takes the initiative. The fecundity of this history comes from this exchange of dialogical love which challenges the diabolical rupture of the beginning.'[2]

DIALOGUE INVOLVES MUTUAL RESPECT

Real dialogue, says Pierre, demands respect for the conscience and freedom of the other. In dialogue one must not seek to convert the other. recognising 'the many ways to salvation offered by God.'[3] Both Christians and Muslims have been affected by memories from their history which have 'wounded the collective unconscious'.[4] For Christians, in moments of crisis it can be the wars of Allah and the Saracens, or the Moors and the Turks invading Europe, whereas for the Muslims it's the Crusades and colonialism.

Pierre thinks that Christians and Muslims still don't fully respect each other. Christians are proud of their civilisation with its respect for the dignity of the human person, its constant search for new experiences, and its aptitude for business and work. On the other hand, notes Pierre, there is also the destruction which rationalism has left in its wake and its nihilistic attitude towards meaning and values where a Christian culture can no longer flourish. Whereas on the Muslim side they are proud of being ' "the best community" which reminds the world of the place and meaning of God and is committed to respecting his rights in societies ... History shows us that there is not much difference between us in the eyes of the God whom we claim to serve but in fact exploit.'[5]

Mutual respect does not mean that we must hide our true convictions. Ideally, says Pierre, we should be free in dialogue to be completely ourselves without in any way becoming aggressive or compromising our own beliefs. The key Christian revelation is that God is love and consequently the core mission of Christian disciples is to reveal this love to others, to make 'this divine Love contagious by the witness of their life and the sharing of their conviction.'[6] If this is the case then our relationships with Muslims will of necessity be dialogical. Pierre doesn't think that we have yet attained a climate free from various social, political, and religious pressures which would allow such openness and mutual acceptance. For him, real respect for each other implies a certain reciprocity. At present dialogue is often restricted to an exchange of information. Cultural differences make real reciprocity difficult as does the scholastic and deductive nature of much Muslim theology, so different from the inductive, experiential theology of contemporary Christianity.

DIALOGUE THRIVES ON FRIENDSHIP

Because both Christians and Muslims believe that their respective faiths have a universal reach they are inevitably in competition, a competition which can take a polemical form and even lead to violence. Because Muslims understand the *Qur'an* as God's final and definitive revelation to humankind, many find it difficult to accept that they have anything to learn from dialogue with Christianity. As the *Qur'an* comes later than the Jewish and Christian revelation, Muslims see the *Qur'an* as the ultimate and final Word of God. In addition, many Muslims think that because theirs is the final revelation *ipso facto* others will recognise its pre-eminence.

Pierre thinks that these Muslim presuppositions about Jewish and Christian revelation create a barrier to dialogue for 'if reality does not correspond with what the sacred Book [the *Qur'an*] says about it, it is because those Jews and those Christians are unfaithful or in bad faith. The *a priori* vision which one has of the other dispenses one from having recourse to experience and prevents one connecting with reality. This is an essential element of the misunderstandings in which our "dialogue" is becoming perpetually bogged down.'[7]

Pierre tells us that dialogue depends on a mutual welcome. Otherwise, 'each one is alone before the other: there is no encounter or relationship, but submission or exclusion. Each one finds himself

face to face with himself in a loneliness which he has never con-
quered and which nourishes fear of the other and violence. The
breaking of the Covenant, which is in every respect the foundation
of human existence, was synonymous with death in the Bible.'[8] For
Pierre, the mission of the tiny Algerian Church is to enter into dialogue both within the Christian community and with the Muslim
people, thus continuing God's dialogue with humankind which cul-
minated in the incarnation of Jesus.

The quality of its encounters, of its relationships is decisive as the
Algerian Church is almost totally bereft of institutional structures
and organisations: 'The announcement of the Good News can only
be made by and in a dialogue carried out after the manner of Jesus
himself in his encounters and relationships which form the framework of the Gospels. Paul VI wrote again concerning this: "Dialogue
thrives on friendship" (*Ecclesiam Suam*, n. 87).'[9]

Real friendship changes us. Pierre writes: 'We can only enter into
this relationship [of dialogue and friendship] if we are also ready to
receive something from others, to review our easily acquired certainties which haven't been truly assimilated. One doesn't escape
unscathed from dialogue; it obliges us to deepen our identity, not
to remain stuck in our prejudices, our habits, our fixed ideas about
everything and everyone.'[10]

Both sides must face up to the reality of their history and not take
refuge in myths. Both sides have had their moments of glory and
their moments of shame. No one is innocent. Pierre encourages us
to be both frank and truthful: 'One does not build a common existence on half-truths or lies in order to avoid displeasing the other.'[11]

DIALOGUE STARTS WITH A QUESTION

Pierre notes that Christians no longer wish to conquer or dominate
Islam and, in their desire for a rapprochement, now ask themselves
the burning question: Why Islam? What purpose does it serve? 'It

doesn't appear to throw new light on any of the essential points of Christian revelation: we agree on a few of them, we judge it to fall short of [the Christian understanding] on many others. Jesus Christ remains the fulfilment who, by his Passover, allows us to enter into the communion of the Trinity. By the simple fact of its existence, and by its radical questioning of the heart of our faith, Islam obliges us to deepen our convictions, to convert our behaviour so that we can give a better account of our hope.' [12]

Pierre wonders if the Muslim partners in dialogue pose similar questions. Because Muslims are convinced that the *Qur'an* is God's final word to humankind they aren't, for the most part, interested in what Christian revelation has to say. As a result, dialogue has no impact. If each side enters into dialogue convinced that they possess the complete truth then there is nothing to learn from one's inter-locutor, says Pierre. Religion, instead of being a force which impels a person to go out of themselves toward God and others, becomes a barrier to understanding the other. Dialogue demands an openness to a shared search for the truth in which we seek together to answer the vital questions about the meaning of our human condition.[13] This is the opposite, states Pierre, of the dogmatism which knows in advance all the answers and which can quickly become a source of oppression, intolerance and fanaticism.

In a talk given at *Le Mistral,* a diocesan formation and confer-ence Centre, in Marseille in 1993 Pierre remarked that 'the most profound and most profitable dialogue' between Christians and Muslims occurred when both sides were confronting common dif-ficulties. At present, both sides are arrogant and believe that theirs is the superior civilisation destined to rule and that they possess all the truth. It's only when people live side by side that they begin to appreciate each other's strengths and weaknesses and, by facing up to reality, begin to humanise and transform it. Today, says Pierre, we need both the western and Islamic civilisations if we are to find our full humanity and a new equilibrium.

People in Algeria, notes Pierre, became confused and shaken by the different forms of Islam which took root in the country, especially from the 1970s onwards. Muslims who had taken part in wars in the Lebanon, Iran, Sudan and Afghanistan had returned to tell their fellow Algerians that their traditional forms of Islam were no good and that they were bad Muslims, because they didn't pray, or dress or act in a certain manner: 'And this is a deep upheaval which concerns not just details but which asks the fundamental question, who can tell us what is the real Islam.' [14]

With the arrival of the civil war (1992-2002) and the widespread slaughter of innocent people in the name of God, people became even more confused about what the Islamic tradition really taught, and in their uncertainty they became more open to religious dialogue with Christians. Up until then, Islam had been totally identified with the Algerian culture. Now they had begun to ask themselves how it was possible to murder and kill in God's name. Algerians could no longer unquestioningly identify with Islam, says Pierre, but had, for the first time, to make a personal choice as to which kind of Islam they wished to belong: 'Personal choice is now necessary and it is for me the arrival in Algerian society of that which Professor Talbi calls "modernity", the emergence of the individual.' [15]

Prior to this, remarks Pierre, dialogue had usually been initiated by Christians who started from their own concerns about Islam and their own ways of thinking, whereas now Muslims were putting their own questions arising from their own experience and way of looking at the world. This unheard of questioning, and uncertainty about their religious identity, provided an ideal opportunity for real dialogue 'because there can only be a dialogue when there are questions. As long as one has only certainties to exchange, such as mutual information which can be superficially enriching, one is not involved in a common questioning where both sides, because they have been shaken to the core, are searching for a truth which is greater than themselves, than each other. This is how dialogue can be reborn from the upheaval and the ruins of today.' [16]

EVANGELISATION AND DIALOGUE

As a member of the Pontifical Committee for Interreligious Dialogue Pierre had helped to write the Vatican document *Dialogue and Proclamation* (1991). At his *Le Mistral* talk the question was put to him: 'Can the Good News be proclaimed in Algeria today?' In his reply Pierre explained that he saw evangelisation and dialogue as forming a seamless whole:

> Evangelisation is carried out fully by proclamation and by dialogue. Dialogue is a full and integral part of evangelisation. Everything that we live in our relations with Muslims is evangelisation in so far as that which we live, we live it in the name of Jesus Christ, out of love for Jesus Christ and out of love for this people [Algerian]. And the question which the Algerians may ask themselves is: But why do they act in this way? And if there are Algerians who become Christians today, it is not because we have proclaimed [verbally] Jesus Christ but because they have seen the way Christians live. And to a certain extent it's almost a grace for us that we are obliged to remain silent where words are concerned because this obliges us to invest gestures, behaviour, with their full weight of meaning and not to rely solely on words. [17]

Pierre goes on to explain why words are not sufficient on their own in a Muslim cultural context. Words aren't forbidden as such in Algeria, although proselytism is. [18] There is a more compelling reason to beware of evangelisation which relies solely on words and abstract teaching, namely, the different theological understanding and significance which the same words carry for Muslims and Christians:

> Why not words? Not, first of all, because that would be forbid-

den but because we haven't got the words to express our faith, the cultural gap is such between the Arab, Muslim, Maghrebi world and the Christian world that what we say makes no sense. If I proclaim Jesus Son of God, there's a complete blockage, it's totally incomprehensible and a grave blasphemy. And for us that makes no sense either if one understands it in the same way as Muslims do. If the Trinity were actually, as the *Qur'an* describes it in a verse – God, Mary and Jesus ... Well whoever says son says father and mother. Well then, am I going to announce Jesus Christ, Son of God, Saviour of the world? There's no point in doing it. Like St Paul at the Areopagus, it doesn't make any sense. If I say 'Mary the mother of God', it makes things even worse. God himself! And that is why it is important for me to live in the Muslim world. Why? Because it forces me to revise my vocabulary. What does it mean to proclaim the Good News? What does 'Son of God' mean to me? [19]

The blasphemous nature, for Muslims, of some Christian credal affirmations forces Christians to deepen their understanding and summons them to a spiritual awakening without which these affirmations are mere empty formulas.

A SHARED EXPERIENCE AND A SHARED VOCABULARY

This need in Christian-Muslim dialogue for a common vocabulary, rooted in a common experience, was a favourite theme of Pierre's, not merely the same words but words whose meaning are understood clearly by both sides, for even the word 'God' is understood differently by Christians and Muslims. While it is easy to be clear about our principal differences, namely, the triune nature of God, the incarnation and Jesus' saving death on the cross, Pierre was also aware of the possibility of deluding ourselves about the extent to which we hold beliefs and practices in common. The danger lies in using the same words, like 'God', 'revelation', prophet', 'morality/ law', without recognising that these words have different meanings in the theology and spirituality of the other faith.[20]

To learn how to live with the other who is different, to share their experience, requires a willingness to leave oneself behind and to cross boundaries of difference. In order for words to have the same meaning, it is necessary to live, to share a common experience, the experience of birth, life, suffering, death: 'To give words their weight of flesh, for me that is what dialogue means.'[21] This is what the in-carnation means, says Pierre. Jesus took on flesh in a particular lo-cation among a specific people. Likewise, they are Christians in a particular country, Algeria, and among a specific people, Algerians:

> So I tell myself, we must learn again to talk, we must learn
> again common words, we must sort out again our vocabu-
> lary, we must shape words which are carried by a common
> experience; and that's why I believe that all dialogue can only
> be embedded in a shared life where, together, we do our best
> to live, where we try to take up together common challenges
> which aren't always religious. But in this common existence,
> we shape the words which say what we are and in what we
> believe. They don't merely repeat the standard discourse. It's
> in this sense that I plead for dialogue. Yes, I believe that all
> of our life is meant for that, a dialogue which is a sharing of
> experiences in which the words to mutually express ourselves
> can begin to be born.[22]

PERSEVERING TOGETHER

In the aftermath of the Second Vatican Council, Catholics took part in the first big Christian-Muslim encounters at Cordova in 1974 and 1977 and in many other gatherings which followed in subsequent years. While these forums allowed people to get to know each other, unfortunately, says Pierre, very little progress was made. The par-

ticipants lacked a common vocabulary to express their core beliefs:
'Very quickly people became disillusioned; there wasn't a good rap-
port. If it were still possible to make friendships, it remained difficult to understand each other's reasons for living and believing.
We weren't still purified enough from the desire to dominate the
other.'[23] Pierre is convinced that only patient working together outside the limelight and free from all pressure, like the work carried
out by the Islamo-Christian Research Group (*Groupe de Recherches
Islamo-Chrétien,* GRIC), can produce fruit. As a result of four years
of working together, the necessary mutual respect, trust and friendship were acquired in order to produce a joint book on how Christians and Muslims understand their scriptures,[24] a text which contained the spirit and language of true dialogue.

   This concept of dialogue is a fresh way of expressing what is usually referred to as the 'dialogue of life' where people get to know each
other as neighbours; and the 'dialogue of action' where Christians
and Muslims deepen their friendship through working together for
the common good of society. It is in this context of a lived experience of each other and, better still, in a common cause that barriers
of fear and misunderstanding can be broken down and prejudices
laid to rest. And, as Pierre points out above, a common vocabulary
can be minted. We have need of each other to flourish both as individuals and as communities. Pierre comments: 'When a people or a
human group chooses to live in isolation – or is ostracised – through
racial, cultural, political or religious segregation then violence is
close.'[25]

NO ONE POSSESSES THE WHOLE TRUTH

Objective truths do exist, says Pierre, but they are not the personal
possession of any individual or group; they are greater than them
and we have all got to set out in search of them. Pierre sees the Catholic Church's position as having evolved in four stages: 'Basically,

the Church has followed historically the stages which characterise the convictions of new believers. Four have been noted: i) the received truth is the only one, this is the era of exclusion; ii) it must be shared, this is conquest and mission; iii) it cannot be [shared] totally, this is the era of negative tolerance; iv) finally, this truth also exists in the other, this is the era of positive tolerance. I am convinced that the slow birth of a concrete truth cannot skip these stages which constitute so many necessary insights.'[26]

No one possess the whole truth, states Pierre: 'We have need of one another: the other has something to teach me which I still lack today.'[27] As a Christian, Pierre believes that Jesus reveals in all its fullness the Truth of God and of humankind. However, he doesn't claim to possess the mystery of Jesus which is being continuously revealed down through the ages as our understanding of the spiritual, human and scientific worlds grows. Pierre also thinks that others outside the Christian faith can help us to deepen our understanding and awareness of our Christian heritage. He writes: 'The recognition of the action and presence of Jesus in other religions encourages us to respect them. And if the mystery of Christ is also present in them, we can receive new light upon our own revelation which has not yet been completely discovered or understood.'[28]

For Pierre, dialogue isn't an optional extra but an essential component of a living Christian faith. Christian revelation is predicated upon the belief and the experience that God, down through the ages, has initiated a dialogue, a conversation, with the human race, a dialogue which reached its climax in the incarnation. As members of Christ's body we carry on that dialogue both with God and with our fellow human beings, of all religions and of none: 'Dialogue is a task which we must constantly begin again: it alone allows us to disarm fanaticism in ourselves and in others. It is through it that we are called to express our faith in the love of God which will have the last word in face of all the powers of division and death.'[29] Pierre believed that it is only in and through dialogue that we can grow closer to God, the source of all truth, and closer to our neighbour made in the image and likeness of that same God: 'Our faith ... teaches us to discover in others the riches which the Creator has brought to birth, an infinite variety of cultural and spiritual riches. Every people, every culture, every religion contains a part of the mystery of life, a divine mystery which can never be completely comprehended by any of them.' [30]

Epilogue

Mohamed Bouchikhi

Epilogue

A Love Stronger than Death
Pierre and Mohamed

IN UPHOLDING the right to be different, to be part of a 'plural humanity' in a bitterly divided Algeria, Pierre knew that his refusal to be silenced would, in all likelihood, cost him his life. On the evening of the first of August 1996, Pierre was met at Oran airport by a police escort and by Mohamed Bouchikhi, a young Muslim who was helping out over the summer at the Bishop's House. On reaching home, as they crossed the threshold there was a powerful explosion. Pierre and Mohamed were killed instantly, their blood mingled in death. Death had not taken either by surprise. Both of them had willingly and knowingly put their lives at risk, Pierre out of love for a Muslim people and Mohamed out of love for his Christian friends.

Who was Mohamed? And why was he willing to run the risk of being assassinated on account of his friendship with Pierre? Mohamed Bouchikhi was the second of eight children and the oldest male member of his family. He was a native of Sidi-Bel-Abbès where his family lived next door to the presbytery and the convent. Mohamed became great friends with the parish priest, Fr René You. He liked to help out in any way he could, always asking the same

I draw on my book, *Dialogue of the Heart: Christian-Muslim Stories of Encounter* (Dublin: Veritas, 2015), pp. 119-135, for some of the material in this chapter.

question: 'Do you need anything?' His personality, according to Fr René, could be seen above all in his eyes 'which radiated permanently a smile, gentleness, the greatness of his soul or the breadth of his heart.'[1] When Mohamed's father evicted the whole family from their home, Fr René gave them refuge in the presbytery for a year. And no doubt this great act of generosity further strengthened Mohamed's friendship with the Christian community.

In the summer of 1996 the handyman at the Bishop's residence was on holiday and 21-year-old Mohamed willingly responded to Mgr Claverie's request that he should take his place. On hearing from Fr René that Mohamed was going to help out over the summer, Mgr Claverie confided to him: 'You know, if only for a man like Mohamed, it's worth the trouble of staying on in this country, even at the risk of one's life.'[2] Mohamed knew that he was putting his life on the line. Just a few months earlier the seven monks of Tibhirine had been kidnapped and beheaded. On agreeing to become Pierre's helper he had said: 'I'm doing it because I love you, but I'm going to be killed.'[3] Unfortunately, Mohamed's premonition was to be fulfilled.

A RUNAWAY SUCCESS

The life and witness of Pierre and that of the other 18 Algerian martyrs live on in surprising ways. No one could have predicted that a play written by Br Adrien Candiard OP, *Pierre & Mohamed*, about the friendship between Pierre and his young driver, Mohamed, would prove to be a runaway success. The dialogue between Pierre and Mohamed is played by a single actor with, from time to time, some heightening of the atmosphere being provided by some music on the hang, also known as the hang drum. Each character reflects in turn upon what it means to engage in dialogue and share friendship with the other.

The play was first staged, to critical acclaim, at the Avignon

Festival in 2011. Since then it has toured the length and breadth of France and elsewhere to full houses. On 13 May 2016 the 621st performance[4] was staged in the *Centre Pierre Claverie* in Oran as part of a two-day colloquium commemorating the twentieth anniversary of Pierre's assassination. Present were Mohamed's mother, Mme Zouaouia Bouchikhi and Pierre's sister, Mrs Anne-Marie Gustavson-Claverie. At the colloquium, Mgr Henri Teissier, emeritus Archbishop of Algiers, and a close friend of Pierre's, spoke about the reasons for the play's continuing success, foremost among them being its topicality and the importance of the issues which it highlights.[5]

Br Adrien portrays Mohamed as someone who recognises Pierre's love for him and for the Algerian people. Mohamed wants to understand the nature and the 'why' of this gratuitous love which astounds and puzzles him. Br Adrien, in writing the play, drew on the homilies and writings of Mgr Claverie. He also made use of the short account of Mohamed's life provided by Fr René in *La vie spirituelle* and of some other references to Mohamed in the same periodical. Br Adrien succeeds brilliantly in portraying the spontaneity of Mohamed, his freshness of spirit, and his innocent goodness. The unexpected success of the play in France and elsewhere is due, I think, to the sensitivity of Br Adrien who succeeded in finding the right words with which to convey a sense of the Holy Spirit at work in their relationship. Both Pierre and Mohamed lived out with integrity the 'sacrament of encounter'.

A TIME FOR FRIENDSHIP

Br Adrien didn't draw upon the notebook left by Mohamed which only contained, according to Br Adrien, 'patchy notes, written in Algerian Arabic (but in Latin characters) often almost unintelligible.'[6] The spiritual Testament written carefully in Arabic a few days before his death is, on the contrary, a precious document. Mohamed's final

Testament allows us to discover the richness of his inner life and shows clearly that he was offering his life freely out of love for his Christian friends. The key words are 'peace', 'thanks', 'forgiveness', and the text is suffused by a feeling of gratitude for all that life had given him. His God is a God of 'omnipotence' and of 'tenderness'.

What is the secret of the relationship between Pierre and Mohamed? It lies, I think, in a reciprocal love which recognises their fundamental equality. Any real friendship implies a relationship of equality. And both of them succeeded in this challenging task in a country where the former relationship of coloniser/colonised, superior/inferior, still rankles in the collective memory. Pierre Claverie knew that the key pre-condition for a fruitful dialogue was friendship. In the play, Br Adrien has Mohamed speak these words attributed to Pierre: 'Dialogue cannot start yet, he said to me, because before dialogue can begin, there has to be a time of friendship. He had come to Algeria to live out a friendship which makes possible a true word, a word which listens, which doesn't deny the other by trying to convince them.'[7]

But, in the long run, if this friendship is to succeed both will need to assume their own identity: 'To discover the Other, live with the Other, hear the Other, to be shaped by the Other, that doesn't mean losing one's identity, rejecting one's values, it means envisaging a plural humanity, without exclusion.'[8] This capacity to accept the other in all their difference and uniqueness allows mutual love to flourish. Pierre exclaims: 'If I only see you as a Muslim, and if you only see me as a Christian, then I can no longer encounter Mohamed and you will never know Pierre. And I will never succeed in understanding who you are, nor how you pray to God.'[9] In other words, the foundation of all dialogue and of all human relationships is the recognition of the humanity of the other. The 'plural humanity', of which Pierre speaks, recognises the unity and the complementarity of the human race, despite differences of colour, religion or culture.

A WOUNDED CONSCIENCE

How did Mohamed, still only 21, manage to overcome all those religious and cultural barriers in his friendship with Pierre and the Christian community, surrounded as he was by violence, hatred and extremism on all sides? Where did he find the confidence and the love to forge a relationship stronger than death?

The assassination of the seven Tibhirine monks on 21 May 1996 had a big impact on him. He told Fr François Chavanes OP that on hearing the news he had gone with a friend to the coast road to look at the sea and shed tears for the monks.[10] Mohamed's conscience was wounded by this barbarity and by the other terrible acts of savagery committed by Islamists in the name of Islam, an Islam which he didn't recognise. He told Andrée Ghillet: 'For four years I have no longer said "*bismillah*" [In the name of Allah] because they slit people's throats in the name of God. For four years I have no longer said "*hamdullah*" [Praise be to Allah], for how can one give thanks to God when there are queues, unemployment and rising prices?'[11] Mohamed didn't go to the mosque but, as his journal shows, he did pray and meditate privately.

The key to understanding Mohamed's personality and motivation can be found in his final Testament. Knowing that his life was in danger, Mohamed, shortly before his assassination, wrote this brief document. In it he shows a spiritual maturity and sensitivity beyond his years. Mohamed had been tried in the crucible of suffering. This suffering had not destroyed him because he had also known what it meant to be loved: loved by God, loved by his mother and family, and loved also by Fr René, Pierre and the Christian community. And this love had empowered him to offer his life for others. In his friendship with Fr René and the sisters of Sidi-Bel-Abbès, and later with Pierre, Mohamed must have glimpsed the 'tenderness' of God to which he refers in his Testament. And he responded faithfully to this experience with the gift of his life.

Peace Be With You

In the Name of God, the Clement, the Merciful One

Before taking up my pen, I say to you: Peace be with you. I thank you who will read my diary and I offer my thanks to everyone who has known me in my life. I say that they will be rewarded by God on the last day. Farewell to anyone to whom I may have done harm, may they forgive me. May whoever forgives me be forgiven on the Day of Judgement; and whoever I may have harmed may he forgive me. I ask forgiveness from anyone who has heard me say a wicked word, and I ask all my friends to forgive me on account of my youth. However, on this day on which I am writing to you, I remember all the good things which I have done in my life. May God, in his omnipotence, grant me the gift of obedience to Him and may He bestow on me his tenderness.[12]

A QUESTION OF LOVE

Mohamed, who had not known the compromises and the betrayals of adulthood, was willing to lay down his life in fidelity to his friendship with the Christian community. Fr René You poignantly describes Mohamed's funeral cortège: 'What more can one say? Except that he, of the Muslim tradition, after having mingled his blood with that of a Christian, was led to the Sidi-Bel-Abbès cemetery by an unexpected crowd of young people, men and women for whom, even the day before, he was still only a stranger.'[13]

I will leave the final word to Pierre, taken from his last homily outside Algeria on 23 June 1996, at Prouilhe, the birthplace of the Dominican Order, which he was visiting for the first time. Less than two months before his assassination, Pierre insists that the Church must always be at the foot of the Cross, sharing the suffering of the most abandoned:

For here it is really a question of love, love first of all and love alone. A passion for which Jesus has given us the taste and shown the way: 'There is no greater love than to lay down one's life for those whom one loves'. [14]

It was fitting that Pierre should die with a Muslim friend. Their blood, mingled in death, gives the lie to all those who claim that Christians and Muslims are doomed to live at enmity with one another. Both Mohamed and Pierre freely lay down their lives for each other, for Christian-Muslim friendship. Their witness continues to bear much fruit. In the words of the psalmist: 'Their voice goes out through all the earth, and their words to the end of the world' (Psalm 19:4).

Appendix

Announcement of the Beatification of 19 of Our Brothers and Sisters

Statement from the Bishops of Algeria

It's a time of rejoicing for our Church. Pope Francis has just authorised the signing of the Decree of Beatification of Bishop Pierre Claverie and his 18 Companions. We have been given the grace of being able to remember our 19 brothers and sisters as martyrs, that is to say (according to the meaning of the word itself) witnesses to the greatest love, that of giving one's life for those whom one loves. Facing the ever-present danger of death, they made the choice, risking their lives, to steadfastly maintain to the end the bonds of fellowship and friendship which they had forged with their Algerian brothers and sisters. The bonds of fellowship and friendship were even stronger than the fear of death.

Our brothers and sisters would not be happy for us to set them apart, separate from those among whom they gave their lives. They are witnesses to a fraternity which knows no frontiers, to a love which makes no distinctions. That is why their death shines a light

My translation is an emended version (based on the original French) of the Algerian Bishops' translation. I also consulted a translation by Anne-Marie Gustavson, the sister of Mgr Pierre Claverie.

The Certainty of Being Loved

on the martyrdom of so many others: Algerians, Muslims, those
searching for meaning, peacemakers, those persecuted for justice,
decent men and women who remained faithful unto death during
that blood-soaked black decade in Algeria.

Our thoughts also reach out in a similar tribute to all our other
Algerian brothers and sisters – and there are thousands of them –
who also were not afraid to risk their lives by remaining true to their
faith in God, to their country and to their conscience. Among them
we remember the 99 imams who lost their lives because they refused
to endorse violence. We think of the intellectuals, the writers, the
journalists, the scientists and artists, members of the security forces
and all those humble, anonymous mothers and fathers who refused
to obey the orders of the armed groups. A number of children also
lost their lives, engulfed by the same violence.

We can focus on the life of each one of our 19 brothers and sisters. Every one of them died because, by the grace of God, they had
chosen to remain faithful to those whom they had befriended in
their neighbourhood through daily encounters and mutual service.
Their deaths show that their lives were at the service of all: the poor,
women in difficulty, handicapped people, young people – all of
them Muslims. A vicious ideology, a deformation of Islam, couldn't
tolerate those who were of a different nationality or faith. Those
who suffered the most at the time of their tragic deaths were their
Muslim friends and neighbours, distressed that the name of Islam
should be used to justify such acts.

But today we are not facing towards the past. These beatifications
are a light for our present and our future. They tell us that hatred is
not the right way to react to hatred, that there isn't an inevitable spi-
ral of violence. They wish to enable everyone to take a step towards
forgiveness and peace, starting with Algeria but extending beyond
its borders. They are a prophetic word for our world, for all those
who believe in and strive for harmony. And they are many, here in
our country and throughout the world, of every nationality and of

every religion. This is the deeper meaning behind Pope Francis' decision. More than ever, our shared home, this planet of ours, needs that rich and beautiful humanity of all of us.

These brothers and sisters of ours are also models for us on the path of everyday holiness. They are witnesses that a life which is simple, yet totally given to God and to others, can lead to the heights of the human vocation. They are not heroes. They didn't die for an idea or for a cause. They were simply members of the small Catholic Church in Algeria – made up mainly of foreigners and often looked upon as being foreign – who embraced the consequences of its choice to belong completely to this country. It was clear to every one of its members that when one loves someone one doesn't abandon them in their hour of need. This is the daily miracle of friendship and fellowship. Many of us knew them and lived with them. Today their lives belong to all. From now on they accompany us as pilgrims of friendship and of universal brotherhood.

Algiers, 27 January 2018

✠ Paul Desfarges, Archbishop of Algiers
✠ Jean-Paul Vesco, Bishop of Oran
✠ John MacWilliam, Bishop of Laghouat
✠ Jean-Marie Jehl, Administrator of Constantine

....

Notes

FOREWORD

1 Jean-Jacques Pérennès OP, *A Life Poured Out* (Maryknoll New York: Orbis Books, 2007), p. 163, translated by Phyllis Jestice and Matthew Sherry from *Pierre Claverie, Un Algérien par alliance*.
2 Op. cit., p. 220.

PREFACE

1 Message of Pope Francis for the Beatification of the Martyrs Msgr Pierre Claverie, OP, Bishop of Oran, and 18 Companions (men and women religious) in Algeria: http://w2.vatican.va/content/francesco/en/messages/pont-messages/2018/documents/papa-francesco_20181202_messaggio-beatificazione-algeria.html
2 Jean-Jacques Pérennès, *Pierre Claverie, Un Algérien par alliance* (Paris: Les Èditions du Cerf, 2000), p. 67, letter on 20 September 1959.
3 Pierre Claverie, *Je ne savais pas mon nom: Mémoires d'un religieux anonyme* (Paris : Les Éditions du Cerf, 2006), p. 52.
4 Pierre Claverie, *Lettres et messages d'Algérie*, édition revue et augmentée, (Paris : Éditions Karthala, 1996), p. 149.
5 *Le Lien*, "La face humaine de Dieu', octobre, 1982.

CHAPTER 1 COLONIAL BACKGROUND

1 Pierre Claverie, 'Itinéraire', *La vie spirituelle*, n° 721, octobre 1997, pp. 723-724.
2 See Benjamin Stora, *Algérie, histoire contemporaine*, 1830-1988, (Alger: Casbah Editions, 2004), p. 14.
3 Claudine Robert-Guiard, Presses universitaire de Provence, accessed on 29 October, 2017: http://books.openedition.org/pup/7084?lang=en
4 Ibid.
5 Ibid.
6 Pierre Claverie, *Il est tout de même permis d'être heureux, Lettres familiales 1967-69* (Paris: Les Éditions du Cerf, 2003), p. 537, 9 February 1969. [Henceforth *Il est tout de même…*]
7 Marie Cardinal, *Au pays de mes racines*, (Paris: Grasset, 1980), pp. 52-53.
8 Alistair Horne, *A Savage War of Peace: Algeria 1954-1962* (New York: New York Review Books, 2006), p. 35.
9 Op. cit., p. 34.
10 See Stora, op. cit., pp. 109-110.
11 Horne, p. 24.

12 Le Monde et E. J. L., *La guerre d'Algérie, 1954-1962*, Document (Paris: Libro, 2004), p. 17.
13 Stora, p. 95.
14 Horne, op. cit., p. 28.
15 See https://www.youtube.com/watch?v=OCxS3wXob3Y, accessed 28 February 2018.
16 It was only in 2005 that the French ambassador to Algeria, Hubert Colin de Verdière, apologised for the Sétif massacre. Speaking at Sétif on February 27, 2005, he described the repression and indiscriminate killing of thousands of civilians as a 'massacre' and 'an inexcusable tragedy.'
17 See Horne, op. cit., pp. 69-73.
18 Mouloud Feraoun, *Journal: 1955-1962* (Paris : Éditions du Seuil, 1962).
19 Op. cit., p. 45. On 15 March 1962, less than four months before Independence Day, Mouloud Feraoun, along with five others, was taken out of a meeting and assassinated by an OAS death squad. On that hate filled day Algeria lost one of its greatest writers and finest human beings. The OAS, *Organisation armée secrète*, (Secret Army Organisation) was an illegal paramilitary group, founded in 1961, which sought by force to keep Algeria under French rule.
20 Jean-Jacques Pérennès, *Pierre Claverie, Un Algérien par alliance*, p. 80.
21 *Il est tout de même...*, p. 353.
22 Interview with Pierre Claverie in *Chemins de Dialogue*, Numéro 29, (Marseille: Juin 2007), p. 142, first published in *La Revue du Rosaire*, juillet 1991.
23 Pierre Claverie, *Quel Bonheur d'être croyant!: Vie religieuse en terre algérienne*, (Paris: Les Éditions du Cerf, 2012), pp. 53-54.
24 Pierre was a novice in Lille from December 1958 until December 1959 and pursued his theological studies at *Le Saulchoir* near Paris from 1959-67, apart from time spent on military service in Algeria.
25 *Quel Bonheur d'être croyant!*, pp. 55-56.
26 Op. cit., pp. 26-27.
27 Letter to parents 29 February 1960, in the possession of his sister Anne-Marie.

CHAPTER 2 **A UNITED FAMILY**

1 Anne-Marie Gustavson-Claverie, 'Après la communion : messages et témoignages', *La vie spirituelle*, n° 721, octobre 1997, p. 600.
2 Pierre Claverie, 'Itinéraire', *La vie spirituelle*, n° 721, octobre 1997, p. 724.
3 *Il est tout de même...*, p. 246.
4 Information contained in an e-mail from Pierre's sister, Anne-Marie, to author on March 15, 2018.
5 Pierre Claverie, *Cette contradiction continuellement vécue, Lettres familiales 1969-75* (Paris: Les Éditions du Cerf, 2007) p. 362. [Henceforth, *Cette contradiction...*].
6 Op. cit., p. 423.
7 *Pierre Claverie, Un Algérien par alliance*, pp. 60-61. An English translation is also available: *A Life Poured Out : Pierre Claverie of Algeria* (New York: Orbis Books, 2007).
8 *Il est tout de même...*, p. 582.
9 Op. cit., p. 426.
10 Op. cit., p. 527.
11 Op. cit., p. 577.
12 At the time of writing (2018) three volumes of Pierre's letters covering the years 1967-1981 have been published and I have made extensive use of them in Part 1 of this book. A fourth volume of his letters, 1958-1967, written while he was training to be a Dominican friar and priest, is being prepared for publication by his sister and brother-in-law.

The majority of the letters are between Pierre and his father with a small number being written by his mother, sister and brother-in-law. For the most part the letters outline the daily events in the lives of the writers but they also contain reflections of a more general nature, especially regarding developments in the post-conciliar Church.

13 *Cette contradiction…*, p. 102.
14 E-mail to author on 28 January 2018.
15 Ibid.
16 *Il est tout de même…*, p. 580.
17 *Un Algérien par alliance*, p. 85.
18 *Cette contradiction…*, p. 320.
19 Pierre Claverie, 'La vie naît de l'amour, elle renaît de la confiance et de la miséricorde', *La vie spirituelle*, n° 721, octobre 1997, p. 790.
20 E-mail to author on 17 February 2018.
21 *Un Algérien par alliance.*, p. 25.
22 Jean-Jacques Pérennès (sous la direction de), *Pierre Claverie: La fécondité d'une vie donnée* (Paris: Les Éditions du Cerf, 2018), p. 93.
23 *Cette contradiction…*, p. 468.
24 *Pierre Claverie, Là où se posent les vraies questions, Lettres familiales 1975-1981* (Paris: Les Éditions du Cerf, 2012) p. 174. [Henceforth, *Là où se posent…*].
25 Redouane Rahal, 'Hommages à un ami disparu prématurément et brutalement', *La vie spirituelle*, n° 721, octobre 1997, p. 623.
26 *Un Algérien par alliance*, p. 383.
27 *Il est tout de même…*, p. 84.
28 *Un Algérien par alliance*, p. 327.
29 *Il est tout de même…*, p. 133.
30 The quotations which follow are taken from replies to my e-mail questionnaire in French in January 2018.
31 *Maître*: a title given to lawyers.
32 *Un Algérien par alliance*, p. 86.

CHAPTER 3 **A TIME OF SPIRITUAL AWAKENING**

1 Pierre Claverie, 'Le frère prêcheur sera l'homme de la sortie de l'esclavage et de la suffisance arrogante… Comme Jean-Baptiste', *La vie spirituelle*, n° 721, octobre 1997, p. 796.
2 Jean-Jacques Pérennès (sous la direction de), *Pierre Claverie: La fécondité d'une vie donnée*, p. 92.
3 Op. cit., p. 92.
4 Op. cit., p. 93.
5 *Un Algérien par alliance*, p. 38, homily 1988.
6 Letter to his parents, 20 October 1958, in the possession of his sister Anne-Marie.
7 *Un Algérien par alliance*, p. 57
8 Op. cit., p. 58.
9 Op. cit., p. 59.
10 Op. cit., p. 67.
11 Op. cit., pp. 66-67.
12 Op. cit., p. 67, letter on 20 September 1959.
13 Op. cit., p. 77.
14 When Pierre started his studies they were under a cloud and so he didn't hear them speak at *Le Saulchoir* until 1963.

15 *Un Algérien par alliance* p. 78.
16 Letter to his parents, 14 February 1965, in the possession of his sister Anne-Marie.
17 *Un Algérien par alliance*, p. 78, letter to parents, 22 March 1964.
18 Archives, Oran, 79.01, now published as Pierre Claverie, *Un amour plus fort que la mort: Sur les pas de saint Paul* (Paris, Les Éditions du Cerf, 2018).
19 Archives, Oran, 79.01, *Avec Saint Paul, 1992*, Retraite XV, final version, p. 19.
20 *Un amour plus fort que la mort: Sur les pas de saint Paul*, p. 72.
21 Letter to parents, February 27, 1963, in the possession of his sister Anne-Marie.
22 *Pierre Claverie, Un Algérien par alliance*, p. 63.
23 Pierre Claverie, 'Lettre du Frère Pierre Claverie à ses frères dans l'Ordre à l'occasion de sa nomination épiscopale', *La vie spirituelle*, n° 721, octobre 1997, p. 692.
24 Art. cit., p. 693.
25 Pierre Claverie, 'Itinéraire', *La vie spirituelle*, n° 721, octobre 1997, p. 725.

CHAPTER 4 LIFE AS A DOMINICAN FRIAR

1 *Quel bonheur d'etre croyant*, p. 17, addressed to apostolic Dominican sisters.
2 *Je ne savais pas mon nom: Mémoires d'un religieux anonyme*, p. 172.
3 In a letter to his parents in March 1964 from the Dominican house of studies, *Le Saulchoir*, near Paris, Pierre, tongue in cheek, described the typical Dominican as follows: 'If one were to caricature the psychological tendencies (taken to an extreme) the Dominican would be paranoiac ... As for the definition of paranoiac, above all don't believe the *Petit Larousse*: in fact it is someone who has invested his affectivity in his intellectual life (and often his aggressivity about ideas is proof of this); in turn a seductive or aggressive guy, he is always sure of being the winner; this makes for insufferable guys very difficult to govern. If push comes to shove, I'd willingly believe it...'. It would be inappropriate for a Benedictine to comment on how much truth this description contains!
4 *Il est tout de même...*, p. 55, 17 July 1967.
5 *Cette contradiction...*, p. 541.
6 Op. cit., pp. 502-503.
7 The Protestant pastor, Pierre Rochat, even asked Pierre to stand in for him during the month of August while he was away on holiday!
8 All e-mail quotations in this chapter are taken from responses to my January 2018 questionnaire.
9 *Il est tout de même...*, p. 458.
10 *Cette contradiction...*, pp. 564-565.
11 Op. cit., p. 154.
12 Op. cit., p. 420.
13 *Je ne savais pas mon nom: Mémoires d'un religieux anonyme*, p. 140.
14 *Il est tout de même...*, pp. 76, 77.
15 *Quel Bonheur d'être croyant! : Vie religieuse en terre algérienne*, p. 218.
16 Pierre found his main source of rest and renewal in holidays with his family.
17 Practically all of these retreats have been published by the French Dominican publishing house, Les Éditions du Cerf, Paris. In a work of supreme devotion, the retreat conferences have been carefully edited by Sr Anne-Catherine Meyer OP, a nun at Orbey monastery in France. In exploring Pierre's spirituality, I draw heavily upon these conferences in Part 2 of this book.
18 For example, *Quel Bonheur d'être croyant! : Vie religieuse en terre algérienne*, p. 232.
19 *Petit traité de la rencontre et du dialogue* (Paris : Les Éditions du Cerf, 2001), p. 161.
20 *Cette contradiction...*, p. 453.

CHAPTER 5 **THE CHALLENGES OF AN EVANGELICAL LIFE**

1 *Quel Bonheur d'être croyant! : Vie religieuse en terre algérienne*, p. 141.
2 Op. cit., pp. 147-148.
3 Op. cit., p. 131.
4 Op. cit., p.137.
5 Maître Eckhart, *Conseils spirituels* (Paris: Éditions Payot et Rivages, 2003), p. 74.
6 Pierre Claverie, *Marie la vivante: Sept jours de retraite avec Marie* (Paris : Les Éditions du Cerf, 2006), pp.165-166. Retreat given in 1988.
7 *Je ne savais pas mon nom*, p. 71.
8 Op. cit., p. 72.
9 *Quel Bonheur d'être croyant! : vie religieuse en terre algérienne*, p. 62.
10 See Lk 19:16-31.
11 *Quel Bonheur d'être croyant! : Vie religieuse en terre algérienne*, p. 159.
12 See 2 Cor. 12:7.
13 Op. cit., p. 161.
14 Op. cit., p. 164.
15 The Dominican friars,at profession, make only one promise to the Master of the Order, namely, obedience. However, they do so according to their Constitutions which bind them to the other two evangelical counsels of poverty (or simplicity of lifestyle) and chastity.
16 See *Je ne savais pas mon nom: Mémoires d'un religieux anonyme*, p. 133.
17 Op. cit., p. 120.
18 *Quel Bonheur d'être croyant! : Vie religieuse en terre algérienne*, p. 236.
19 *Il est tout de même...*, p. 274.
20 Fr Henri was later to be appointed Bishop of Oran and subsequently Archbishop of Algiers.
21 Op. cit., p. 439, 12 November 1968.
22 Fr Timothy Radcliffe OP, 'Dominican Freedom and Responsibility, Towards a Spirituality of Government', Rome, 10 May 1997. Text in Timothy Radcliffe OP, *Sing a New Song: The Christian Vocation*, Dublin, Dominican Publications, 2012 edition, pp. 82-120.
23 *Cette contradiction...*, p. 59.
24 *Là où se posent...*, p. 224.
25 Op. cit., p. 225.
26 *Un Algérien par alliance*, p. 144.
27 *Je ne savais pas mon nom: Mémoires d'un religieux anonyme*, p. 105.
28 Op. cit., p. 106.
29 *Là où se posent...*, p. 627.
30 *Un Algérien par alliance*, p. 87.
31 Op. cit., p. 87.
32 Op. cit., p. 40.
33 Pierre Claverie, 'Lettre du Frère Pierre Claverie à ses frères dans l'Ordre à l'occasion de sa nomination épiscopale', *La vie spirituelle*, n° 721, octobre 1997, p. 692.
34 François Chavanes OP, 'Il n'y a d'humanité que plurielle', *La vie spirituelle*, n° 721, octobre 1997, p. 640.
35 All e-mail quotations in this chapter are taken from responses to my January 2018 questionnaire.

CHAPTER 6 **LEAVING ONE'S WHOLE WORLD BEHIND**

1 *Cette contradiction....*, p. 72.
2 *Un amour plus fort que la mort: Sur les pas de saint Paul*, p. 128.
3 Op. cit., p. 128.
4 Cheikh Claverie, évêque d'Oran: https://videotheque.cfrt.tv/video/cheikh-claverie-eveque-doran/ - accessed 11 March 2018.
5 *Quel Bonheur d'être croyant!: Vie religieuse en terre algérienne*, p. 202.
6 *Il est tout de même...*, p. 141.
7 Op. cit., p. 258.
8 Op. cit., p. 54.
9 *Un Algérien par alliance*, p. 103.
10 *Il est tout de même...*, p. 323.
11 Op. cit., p. 351.
12 Pierre Claverie, *Humanité plurielle* (Paris: Les Éditions du Cerf, 2008), p. 162.
13 *Eid ul-Fitr* which marks the end of Ramadan and *Eid ul-Adha* which remembers Abraham's willingness to sacrifice his son.
14 *Cette contradiction...*, pp. 672-673.
15 Thanks to the vigorous intervention of Cardinal Duval the occupation of the basilicas was brought to an end.
16 *Cette Contradiction...*, p. 766.
17 With the state visit of Queen Elizabeth II to Ireland in May 2011, 90 years after its independence from Britain, the Republic of Ireland could be said to have finally overcome its inferiority complex and acquired the necessary self-confidence to treat Britain as an equal. In all likelihood, it will take Algeria a similar length of time to become self-assured in its relationship with its former colonial master.
18 Surprisingly, the huge and beautiful mosaic of the Risen Christ on the outside of the former cathedral has not been removed and still dominates one of the main streets in the centre of Oran.
19 Pierre Claverie, *Lettres et messages d'Algérie*, édition revue et augmentée (Paris: Éditions Karthala, 1996), p. 91. This book is a collection of editorials written by Pierre for his diocesan magazine *Le Lien* (The Link). When I quote an editorial, if it is contained in this book I give the appropriate page reference. In other cases the reader will need to consult the diocesan archives in order to read the whole editorial.
20 Archives, Oran, dossier 32.00, 'Expérience de notre petite Église au Maghreb'.
21 Op. cit., p. 7.
22 Op. cit., pp. 8, 10.

CHAPTER 7 **TAKING THE SIDE OF THE POWERLESS**

1 Henri Teissier, 'Pierre Claverie, un pasteur pour une Église sans frontière', *La vie spirituelle*, n° 721, octobre 1997, p. 581
2 Pierre Claverie, 'À la rencontre des religions', *La vie spirituelle*, n° 721, octobre 1997, p. 830. This text was originally written for the Forum of Christian Communities at Angers, Pentecost 1994.
3 Pierre Claverie, 'Église en dialogue', *La vie spirituelle*, n° 721, octobre 1997, p. 811. (Forum de Grenoble, April 1996).
4 *Je ne savais pas mon nom: Mémoires d'un religieux anonyme*, p. 159.
5 Op. cit., pp. 159-160.
6 Pierre Claverie, 'Église en dialogue', p. 811.

7   *Cette contradiction...*, p. 416.
8   Op. cit., p. 70.
9   Op. cit., p. 667.
10 Op. cit., pp. 385-386.
11 *Quel Bonheur d'être croyant! : Vie religieuse en terre algérienne*, p. 59.
12 Op. cit., p. 68.
13 E-mail to the author on October 7, 2018.
14 *Là où se posent...*, p. 538.
15 CIMADE – *Comité inter-mouvements auprès des évacués: The inter-movement committee for evacuees.*
16 Pierre Claverie, 'Lettre du Frère Pierre Claverie à ses frères dans l'Ordre à l'occasion de sa nomination épiscopale', *La vie spirituelle*, n° 721, octobre 1997, pp. 693-694.
17 *Petit traité de la rencontre et du dialogue*, p. 146.
18 Pierre Claverie, 'Église en dialogue', *La vie spirituelle*, n° 721, octobre 1997, p. 809. (Forum de Grenoble, April 1996).
19 Art. cit., p. 809.

CHAPTER 8 CONFRONTING THE POWERS OF DARKNESS

1   http://en.wikipedia.org/wiki/Algerian_Civil_War - Wikipedia, Algerian Civil War, 27 October, 2005. The above paragraph is taken from my book *Christian Martyrs for A Muslim People* (New York/Mahwah, NJ: Paulist Press, 2008), p. 19.
2   *Lettres et messages d'Algérie*, édition revue et augmentée, p. 166.
3   Op. cit., p. 166.
4   Op. cit., pp. 113-114.
5   Op. cit., p. 114.
6   Op. cit., p. 104.
7   Pierre Claverie, 'Noël 1994', *La vie spirituelle*, n° 721, octobre 1997, p. 771.
8   The journalist Saïd Mekbel was assassinated for expressing his horror at the assassination in 1994 of two Spanish Augustinian Missionary Sisters, Esther and Caridad.
9   *Lettres et messages d'Algérie*, édition revue et augmentée, p. 166.
10 Op. cit., pp. 151-154.
11 Op. cit., p. 206, *Le Lien*.
12 Op. cit., pp. 153-154.
13 Op. cit., p. 147.
14 Op. cit., pp. 149-150.
15 Op. cit., p. 150.
16 Op. cit., p. 213.
17 Op. cit., p. 217.
18 Op. cit., p. 241.
19 http://www.ina.fr/video/CAB96019550, accessed 12 March 2018.
20 The quotations which follow are taken from answers to my e-mail questionnaire in January 2018.
21 *Il est tout de même...*, p. 458.
22 Eighteen of the 19 priests and religious assassinated between 1994 and 1996 were from the Archdiocese of Algiers where Mgr Teissier was Archbishop. Mgr Claverie was the sole exception.
23 Perhaps the best and most succinct answer to the question of Pierre's prudence or imprudence can be found in Georges Bernanos' *Journal d'un Curé de Campagne* (*The Diary*

of a Country Priest) when M. Le curé de Torcy comments: 'The ultimate imprudence is prudence when it gradually accustoms us to do without God', (London: University of London Press Ltd, 1969), p. 120. 'La dernière des imprudences est la prudence, lorsqu'elle nous prépare tout doucement à nous passer de Dieu.'

24 *Lettres et messages d'Algérie*, édition revue et augmentée, p. 234.

CHAPTER 9 **A SPIRITUALITY OF ENCOUNTER**

1 P. Marius Garau, *La Rose de l'Imam* (Paris: Les Éditions du Cerf), 1983.
2 Op. cit., p. 29.
3 See Luke 4:16-21.
4 *Quel Bonheur d'être croyant!: Vie religieuse en terre algérienne*, p. 270.
5 Christoph Theobald, *Présences d'Évangile: Lire les Évangiles et l'Apocalypse en Algérie et ailleurs* (Paris : Les Editions de l'Atelier), 2003.
6 Op. cit., p. 18.
7 *Lumen Gentium* (no. 1), Austin Flannery OP General Editor, *Vatican Council II: The Basic 16 Documents* (Dublin: Dominican Publications, 1996), p. 1.
8 John Macquarrie, *A Guide to the Sacraments* (London: SCM Press Ltd, 1997), p. 37.
9 *Gaudium et Spes* (no. 22), Flannery, p. 186.
10 Macquarrie, Op. cit., p. 1.
11 See 2 Corinthians 5:20.
12 Philippe Béguerie & Claude Duchesneau, *How to Understand the Sacraments* (London: SCM Press Ltd, 1993), p. 150.
13 *Humanité plurielle*, p. 112, December, 1993.
14 *Le Lien*, août/septembre 1987.
15 *Le Christ et L'Église, Sacrements de la Présence de Dieu dans le Monde*, Archives, Oran, Dossier 20.00, pp. 3-7.
16 Op. cit., p. 4.
17 Op. cit., p. 4.
18 Op. cit., p. 5.
19 Op. cit., p. 5.
20 Theobald, Op. cit., p. 44.
21 *Quel Bonheur d'être croyant! : Vie religieuse en terre algérienne*, p. 243.
22 Theobald, Op. cit., p. 66.
23 Pope Benedict XV1, *Deus Caritas Est*, no. 18.
24 Archives, Oran, Dossier 75, Retraite 1974, *Humanité*, pp. 10-11.
25 Op. cit., p. 12.
26 Op. cit., p. 13.
27 *Là où se posent...*, p. 522.
28 Theobald, op. cit., p. 66.

CHAPTER 10 **DO NOT BE AFRAID, I LOVE YOU**

1 Pierre Claverie et Les Evêques du Maghreb, *Le Livre de la Foi* (Paris: Les Éditions du Cerf, 1996).
2 *Petit traité de la rencontre et du dialogue*, p. 48.
3 Ibid.
4 *Quel Bonheur d'être croyant! : Vie religieuse en terre algérienne*, p. 91.
5 *Humanité plurielle*, p. 231, February 19, 1990.
6 Archives, Oran, *Coran sur Bucaille*, Dossier 53., p. 3, unsigned and undated document.

7   A. J. Droge, *The Qur'an: A New Annotated Translation* (Sheffield: Equinox Publishing Ltd, 2013), p. 198.

8   Pierre Claverie, *Le livre de nos passages: La Bible* (Paris: Les Éditions du Cerf, 2014), pp. 134-135

9   *Verbum Dei*, no. 2, in Austin Flannery OP (editor), *Vatican Council II: Constitutions Decrees, Declarations*, 1996, Dubin, Dominican Publications, p. 98.

10 Archives, Oran, Dossier 75, Retraite 1974, *Humanité*, p. 7.

11 *Le livre de nos passages*, p. 16.

12 Op. cit., p. 20.

13 Op. cit., p. 20.

14 Op. cit., p. 21.

15 Op. cit., p. 36.

16 Op. cit, p. 86.

17 Op. cit., p. 38.

18 Op. cit., p. 95.

19 Op. cit., p. 97.

20 Op. cit., p. 105.

21 Op. cit., p. 109.

22 Op. cit., p. 111.

23 Op. cit., pp. 111-112.

24 *Marie la vivante*, p. 167.

25 *Le livre de nos passages*, p. 49.

26 Archives, Oran, *Coran sur Bucaille*, p. 3.

27 *Le Livre de la Foi*, p. 63.

28 *Petit traité de la rencontre et du dialogue*, p. 61.

29 *Verbum Dei*, no. 2, Flannery, p. 98.

CHAPTER 11 **THERE IS SOMEONE IN HIS LIFE**

1   *Petit traité de la rencontre et du dialogue*, pp. 85-86.

2   Op. cit., p. 86.

3   Op. cit., p. 89.

4   See Matthew 13:53-58.

5   Op. cit., p. 65.

6   Op. cit., p. 67.

7   Mt 7:28-29.

8   *Marie la vivante*, p. 172.

9   Op. cit., p. 176.

10 *Je ne savais pas mon nom: Mémoires d'un religieux anonyme*, p. 22.

11 Op. cit., p. 22.

12 Op. cit., p. 23.

13 Archives, Oran, Dossier 32.00, *Les Derniers et le Règne de l'Homme*, 1995, pp. 32-33.

14 *Petit traité de la rencontre et du dialogue*, p. 72.

15 Archives, Oran, Dossier 75, *La Vie*, 1979, p. 25.

16 *Petit traité de la rencontre et du dialogue*, p. 72.

17 Op. cit., p. 73.

18 Op. cit., p. 76.

19 Op. cit., p. 76.

20 Op. cit., pp. 76-77.

21 Op. cit., p. 77.
22 Op. cit., p. 79.
23 Op. cit., p. 79.
24 Archives, Oran, Dossier 2.02, *Prière*, p. 2, March, 1969.
25 Op. cit., pp. 4-5.
26 Op. cit., p. 5.
27 *Quel Bonheur d'être croyant! : Vie religieuse en terre algérienne*, p. 115.
28 *Petit traité de la rencontre et du dialogue*, p. 130.
29 Op. cit., p. 127.
30 *Je ne savais pas mon nom: Mémoires d'un religieux anonyme*, p. 140.
31 Op. cit., p. 141.
32 Pierre Claverie, 'Église en dialogue', *La vie spirituelle*, n° 721, octobre 1997, p. 809. (Forum de Grenoble, April 1996).

CHAPTER 12 **THE BIRTH OF THE NEW HUMANITY**

1   Archives, Oran, Dossier 79.01, *Avec St Paul*, p. 8.
2   Op. cit., p. 10.
3   *Le Lien*, 'Une Nouvelle Alliance', décembre 1993.
4   Pierre Claverie, *Donner sa vie: Six jours de retraite sur l'Eucharistie*, (Paris: Les Éditions du Cerf, 2003), p. 111.
5   Op. cit., p. 75.
6   See Rom 6:3-4.
7   *Je ne savais pas mon nom: Mémoires d'un religieux anonyme*, p. 52.
8   Op. cit., p. 55.
9   Archives, Oran, Dossier 79.01, *Avec St Paul*, p. 19, footnote 73.
10 Archives, Oran, Dossier 1.01, *Résurrection*, p. 73.
11 *Donner sa vie: Six jours de retraite sur l'Eucharistie*, p. 20.
12 Op. cit., p. 21.
13 Ibid.
14 Op. cit., p. 22.
15 Op. cit., p. 23.
16 Op. cit., p. 24.
17 Op. cit., p. 25.
18 *Je ne savais pas mon nom: Mémoires d'un religieux anonyme*, p. 37.
19 Op. cit., p. 39.
20 Op. cit., p. 39.
21 Op. cit., p. 28.
22 Op. cit., p. 42.
23 *Le Lien*, 'La face humaine de Dieu', octobre 1982.
24 Archives, Oran, Dossier 75, *Béatitudes* (Beatitudes), 1982, p.19.
25 *Le Lien*, 'Chemins de sainteté', novembre 1981.
26 Ibid.
27 *Le Lien*, 'Toussaint: La Vie et la Mort', octobre 1990.
28 Archives, Oran, Dossier 75, Retraites, *Béatitudes bis (8)*, 1982, p. 17.
29 *Là o*ù se posent..., p. 512.

CHAPTER 13 **THE LAW, THE PROPHETS AND GOD**

1   Pierre Claverie, *Petite introduction à l'islam* (Paris: Les Éditions du Cerf, 2010), pp. 65-66.

2   Op. cit., p.86.

3   *Shahada*: the Muslim profession of faith – There is no God but Allah and Mohammed is His Messenger, *Salat*: prayers five times a day, *Zakat*: almsgiving, *Sawm*: fasting during the month of Ramadan, *Hajj*: pilgrimage to Mecca.

4   *Petite introduction à l'islam*, p. 60.

5   Op. cit., p. 61.

6   Op. cit., pp. 18-19.

7   The Catholic approach to morality before the Second Vatican Council had also become very legalistic and he may also have had this in mind.

8   *Lettres et messages d'Algérie*, p. 239.

9   Op. cit., p. 239.

10   Archives, Oran, Dossier 53.00, *Révélation*, Tizi Ouzou, novembre 1980, p. 18.

11   *Le Livre de la Foi*, p. 72.

12   Op. cit., p. 54.

13   Op. cit., p. 80.

14   *Quel Bonheur d'être croyant! : Vie religieuse en terre algérienne*, p. 96.

15   Op. cit, p. 101.

16   François Varillon, *Joie de croire, joie de vivre* (Paris: Bayards Éditions/Centurion, 1981), p. 26.

17   *Quel Bonheur d'être croyant! : Vie religieuse en terre algérienne*, p. 96.

18   Op. cit., p. 96.

19   Op. cit., p. 101.

20   Op. cit., p. 101.

21   Op. cit, p. 92.

22   Op. cit,., p. 92.

23   Op. cit., p. 93.

24   *Petit traité de la rencontre et du dialogue*, p. 124.

25   *Quel Bonheur d'être croyant! : Vie religieuse en terre algérienne*, p. 101.

26   *Le Livre de la Foi*, p.98.

27   See John: 8:32.

CHAPTER 14 **CHRISTIANS AND THE *QUR'AN***

1   Pierre Claverie, 'Lectures du Coran' in *Spiritus*, no. 126, 26 février, 1992, pp. 33-46.

2   Op. cit., pp. 35, 43.

3   See, Archives, Oran, Dossier 53.00, *Coran Hamidullah*, p. 24, lecture notes.

4   *Spiritus*, art. cit., p. 41.

5   Ibid.

6   Art. cit., p. 42.

7   Ibid.

8   *Un amour plus fort que la mort: Sur les pas de saint Paul*, pp. 39-40.

9   *Spiritus*, art. cit., p. 43.

10   Ibid.

11   De Oum El Kheir, 'Après la communion: messages et témoignages', *La vie spirituelle*, n° 721, octobre 1997, p. 604.

12   *Spiritus*, art. cit., p. 44.

13   *Gaudium et Spes*, (no. 22), Flannery, p. 186.

14 *Spiritus*, art. cit., p. 44.
15 Ibid,, quoting from Jacques Dupuis, *Jésus-Christ à la rencontre des Religions* (Paris: Des-clée, 1989) p. 225.
16 *Gaudium et Spes* (no. 22), Flannery, p. 186
17 The above quotations are taken from: Flannery, pp. 570-71 and 458-59.
18 *Christianity and the World Religions*, 1997: http://www.vatican.va/roman_curia/congre-gations/cfaith/cti_documents/rc_cti_1997_cristianesimo-religioni_en.html
19 *Christianity and the World Religions*, no. 42.

CHAPTER 15 CROSSING THE BOUNDARIES OF DIFFERENCE

1 Archives, Oran, 4.01, *Mission de l'Église en Algérie*, 'Une communauté. Une communion', p. 10.
2 See Ephesians 3:18.
3 *Le Lien*, 'Un grand abîme nous sépare', Octobre, 1986. A longer and slightly different version of this editorial is reprinted in *La vie spirituelle*, pp. 783-787.
4 *Quel Bonheur d'être croyant!: Vie religieuse en terre algérienne*, p. 290.
5 Flannery, p. 571.
6 *Address of His Holiness John Paul II to Young Muslims, No. 10*, Casablanca, Morocco, Mon-day, 19 August 1985: can.va/content/john-paul-ii/en/speeches/1985/august/docu-ments/hf_jp-ii_spe_19850819_giovani-stadio-casablanca.html
7 Jean-Jacques Pérennès op, ' "J'ai besoin de la vérité des autres": Dialogue et altérite: La contribution de Pierre Claverie à la réflexion sur le dialogue interreligieux', an unpubli-shed talk given at the *Journées romaines dominicaines* held on the 27-29 September 2018 at the Angelicum University in Rome.
8 *Petit traité de la rencontre et du dialogue*, pp. 35, 36.
9 Archives, Oran, Dossier 75, *Vie religieuse et islam*, 1983, p. 16.
10 *Petit traité de la rencontre et du dialogue*, p. 38.
11 *Le Lien*, 'Un grand abîme nous sépare', octobre, 1986.
12 Ibid.
13 Ibid.
14 *Lettres et messages d'Algérie*, édition revue et augmentée, p. 93.
15 Op. cit., p. 93.
16 Op. cit., pp. 143-144, April, 1994.
17 *Humanité plurielle*, p. 103, November 1987.
18 Op. cit., p. 107.
19 Op. cit., p. 108.
20 *Lettres et messages d'Algérie*, édition revue et augmentée, p. 146, April 1994.
21 *Humanité plurielle*, p. 71, 15 June 1988.
22 Op. cit., p. 54, May 1991.
23 François Varillon, *L'humilité de Dieu* (Paris: Bayard Compact, 2002), p. 795.
24 Archives, Oran, Dossier 93.02, *Semaine de Prière pour l'Unité des Chrétiens*, p. 6.
25 Archives, Oran, Dossier 20.00, *Croire Aujourd'hui, Interview de Pierre Claverie*, p. 37.
26 Archives, Oran, Dossier 20.00, p. 38,
27 *Humanité plurielle*, p. 27.
28 Archives, Oran, Dossier 75, *La Vie 1979*, p. 27.

CHAPTER 16 **PATHWAYS TO DIALOGUE**

1   Pope Paul VI, *Ecclesiam Suam* (No. 70), London: Catholic Truth Society, 1965, p. 42.

2   Pierre Claverie, 'A la rencontre des religions', *La vie spirituelle*, n° 721, octobre 1997, p. 830. This text was originally written for the Forum of Christian Communities at Angers, Pentecost 1994. See also *Humanité plurielle*, pp. 281-285.

3   *Humanité plurielle*, p. 72, 15 June 1988.

4   Op. cit., p. 65.

5   Op. cit., 49, 1985.

6   Op. cit., p. 100, November 1987.

7   Pierre Claverie, 'Chrétiens, musulmans, vivre ensemble ?', *La vie spirituelle*, n° 721, octobre 1997, p. 747. (Lille, 16 January 1992).

8   *Humanité plurielle*, p. 111, December 1993.

9   Op. cit., p. 112.

10   Archives, Oran, 83.00, *Communauté Évangélisatrice*, p. 15, 9 October, 1990.

11   Pierre Claverie, 'Chrétiens, musulmans, vivre ensemble?', p. 750.

12   *Humanité plurielle*, p. 35.

13   Pierre quotes *Nostra Aetate*, No. 1 as an example of some 'vital questions': 'What is humanity? What is the meaning and purpose of life? What is upright behaviour and what is sinful? Where does suffering originate, and what end does it serve? How can genuine happiness be found? What happens at death? What is judgment? What reward follows death? And finally, what is the ultimate mystery, beyond human explanation, which embraces our entire existence, from which we take our origin and towards which we tend?' See Flannery, p. 570.

14   Archives, Oran, *Le Mistral*, 10 January 1993, recorded talk, Cassette 03B1.

15   *Humanité plurielle*, p. 140, January 1996.

16   Ibid., *Le Mistral*. Perhaps we can see the same potential for dialogue arising in the West as moderate Muslims and Christians experience confusion and uncertainty before a growing fundamentalism on both sides.

17   Archives, Oran, *Le Mistral*, 10 January 1993, Cassette 09B2.

18   In 2006 laws were passed in Algeria which impose heavy penalties for proselytism.

19   *Le Mistral*, Cassette 09B2.

20   This issue was explored in Chapter 13.

21   Pierre Claverie, 'Église en dialogue', *La vie spirituelle*, n° 721, octobre 1997, p. 810. (Forum de Grenoble, April 1996).

22   *Humanité plurielle*, p. 11, interview Marseilles, 14 May 1996.

23   Op. cit., p. 75, 15 June 1988.

24   *Ces Écritures qui nous questionnent, la Bible et le Coran* (These Scriptures which question us, the Bible and the Qur'an*),* *(*Paris, Éditions du Centurion, 1987).

25   *Humanité plurielle*, p.27.

26   *Humanité plurielle*, p. 198, 16 April, 1986.

27   Pierre Claverie, 'Chrétiens, musulmans, vivre ensemble?', *La vie spirituelle*, n° 721, octobre 1997, p. 749. (Lille, 16 January 1992).

28   *Le Lien*, 'À la rencontre des religions', octobre 1991.

29   Pierre Claverie, 'Deux homélies du père Pierre Claverie', *La vie spirituelle*, n° 721, octobre 1997, p. 778. (Cathédrale d'Oran, 9 octobre 1981).

30   *Lettres et messages d'Algérie*, édition revue et augmentée, p. 258, 1985.

EPILOGUE **A LOVE STRONGER THAN DEATH**

1 René You, 'À Mohamed', *La vie spirituelle*, n° 721, octobre 1997, p. 572.
2 Art. cit., p. 573.
3 Andrée Ghillet, 'Quelques dattes de Mgr Pierre Claverie', *La vie spirituelle*, n° 721, octobre 1997, p. 667.
4 By November 2018, over 1,200 performances of the play have been staged, mainly in France but also in Algeria, the Lebanon, and Egypt.
5 Bernard Janicot (sous la direction de), *L'actualité de l'œuvre de Pierre Claverie vingt ans après sa mort* (Paris, Les Editions du Cerf, 2017), pp. 29-41.
6 E-mail to author in French on 21 August 2014.
7 Adrien Candiard, *Pierre et Mohamed* (Paris: Tallandier/Éditions du Cerf, 2018), p. 32.
8 Op. cit., p. 25.
9 Op. cit., p. 31.
10 François Chavanes OP, 'Il n'y a d'humanité que plurielle', *La vie spirituelle*, n° 721, octobre 1997, p. 643.
11 Andrée Ghillet, 'Quelques dattes de Mgr Pierre Claverie', p. 667.
12 René You, 'À Mohamed', p. 573.
13 Art. cit., p. 572.
14 Pierre Claverie, 'Dernière homélie à l'étranger, à Prouilhe, berceau de l'Ordre dominicain', *La vie spirituelle*, n° 721, octobre 1997, p. 834.